Also by Nicholas Shrady

Sacred Roads: Adventures from the Pilgrimage Trail

TILT

A Skewed History of the Tower of Pisa

NICHOLAS SHRADY

SIMON & SCHUSTER
NEW YORK   LONDON   TORONTO   SYDNEY   SINGAPORE

SIMON & SCHUSTER
Rockefeller Center
1230 Avenue of the Americas
New York, NY 10020

For information regarding special discounts for bulk purchases,
please contact Simon & Schuster Special Sales at 1-800-456-6798
or business@simonandschuster.com

Designed by Jaime Putorti

Manufactured in China

10   9   8   7   6   5   4   3   2   1

Library of Congress Cataloging-in-Publication Data

 Shrady, Nicholas.
 Tilt : a skewed history of the Tower of Pisa / Nicholas Shrady.
   p. cm.
 Includes bibliographical references.
 1. Leaning Tower (Pisa, Italy). 2. Pisa (Italy)—Buildings, structures,
 etc. 3. Pisa (Italy)—History. I. Title.

 NA5621.P716S55 2003
 945'.55—dc21   2003050460

ISBN 0-7432-2926-6

In loving memory of my parents,
who lived a wonderfully skewed tale of their own

Acknowledgments

I would like to express my gratitude to the following people and organizations for helping me to prepare this book: Christy Fletcher, Denise Roy, David Rosenthal, Eva Ortega, Carlo Quercioli, Josep Mitjavila, Professor John Burland, Gregorio Sánchez, Paige Rense, Paolo Heiniger, Leon Weckstein, the Opera Primaziale Pisana, the British Library, the University of Pisa, UNESCO, Chris and Lesley Cooke, and my sons, Max and Sebastian.

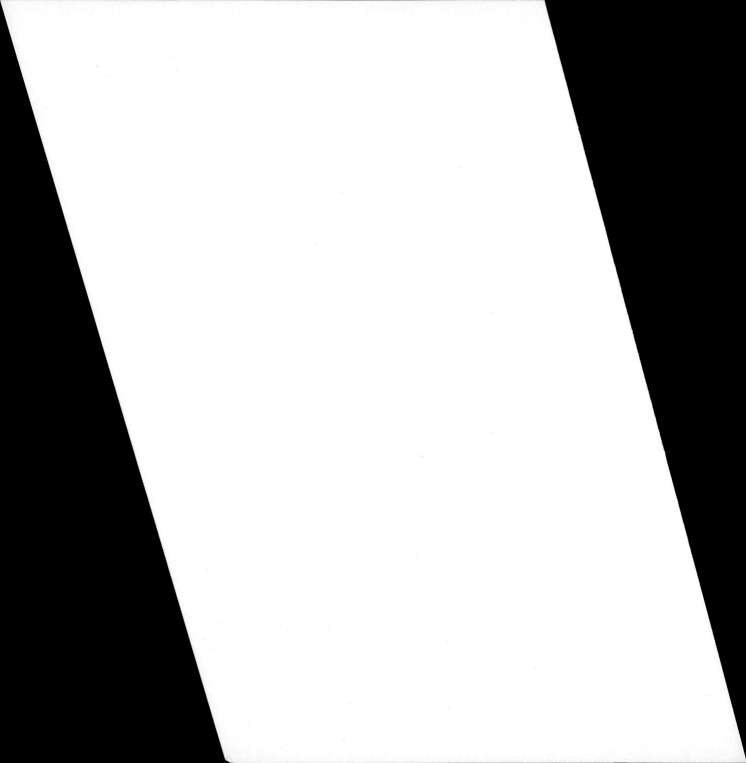

Contents

Introduction

About the tower: as a tower
It is a mere mass of marble and lime;
But eager minds may sometimes wander
And depict the work as divine;
I only venerate the memory of Bonanno,
And would stand by what we know.

—Antonio Guadagnoli d'Arezzo, *Il Campanile di Pisa* (1839)

Out of plumb and off-kilter, the Tower of Pisa is one of those singular monuments which beauty and a sense of bewilderment have conspired to transform into a universal architectural icon. Unlike other wonders of the world both ancient and modern, the Tower of Pisa captures our imaginations for neither the kind of colossal monumentality displayed by, say, the Great Wall of China, nor the sense of hoary otherworldliness surrounding the pyramids at Giza, but rather for its thorough improbability. The tower, currently more than four meters—or five degrees—askew, is the world's most consummate, if unintentional, folly. To stand before the *campanile,* as bell towers are known in Italian, is enough to dispel, at least momentarily, any notion of common sense or the presumably irrefutable laws of physics—as if reality itself is teetering in the finely etched Tuscan light.

Yet for all its power as an architectural marvel, the world's most renowned bell tower is something of a victim of its own notoriety, owing its far-flung reputation to little more than its faulty perpendicular, or, at best, to Galileo Galilei, Pisa's most illustrious native son—who standard science texts and Lives of the Great Scientists tomes invariably depict conducting experiments from the tower's vertiginous heights. What lies behind the tower's pristine white-marble façade and timeworn tourist cliché, however, is a rich cautionary tale of inspired architecture and human machinations, temporal ambitions and spiritual longing, science and superstition, and our persistent urge to gaze in awe at all that is improbable and strange.

Begun in 1173, the campanile has stood as silent witness to the rise and fall of a maritime republic, to victory, glory, treachery, schism, defeat, decadence, and, finally, newfound prominence. The cast of characters who have figured in the tower's tortuous history include Pisan native St. Ranieri, Renaissance politico Niccolò Machiavelli, Galileo, the Renaissance artist and historian Giorgio Vasari, nineteenth-century literati Lord Byron, the Shelleys, and John Ruskin; and such twentieth-century figures as *Il Duce,* Benito Mussolini, German Field Marshal Albert Kesselring, the U.S. Ninety-first Infantry Division, as well as some of the greatest engineers of our time. The tale of the Tower of Pisa is a chronicle of man's relationship with monumental architecture and his irrepressible need first to conceive and build it, and later to appropriate and condition it to suit the tenor of the times.

By all accounts, the Pisan campanile should have toppled long ago. That it has survived the elements, war, ill-advised restoration schemes, and outright human folly does indeed approach the miraculous. Now, a recent decade-long, $30 million effort to stabilize and restore the tower has been widely trumpeted as one of the greatest civil-engineering achievements of our day; according to authorities, this structure that was on the verge of sure ruin will be secure for at least another three hundred years. Let's hope so. The Tower of Pisa, however, is notorious for scorning hope, reason, logic, predictions, and the best intentions; if it were otherwise, in fact, we probably wouldn't stare so intently.

A Pisan Time Line

The origin of ancient Pisae, located on the right bank of the Arno, is lost in the mists of history. We know that the town's first inhabitants were of Ligurian origin, but from the sixth century B.C. onward, the prominent cultural influence in the area was Etruscan. By the third century B.C., Pisae had fallen into the Roman sphere.

180 B.C.	Pisae becomes a Roman colony, Colonia Julia Pisana.
A.D. 300–500 (approx.)	Principal barbarian invasions of Italy.
860	Vikings sack Pisa.
878	Saracens conquer Sicily, taking it from Byzantium.
1003	Pisa goes to war against neighboring Lucca in the first medieval war waged between Italian city-states.
1004	Saracens sack Pisa.
1011	Saracens return but are repulsed by the Pisans. Henceforth, Pisa takes the offensive and scores victories over the Muslims

	in Calabria and southern Italy, Sardinia, North Africa, and Sicily.
1063	Pisa raids Palermo, the capital of Saracen Sicily, and makes off with galleyloads of loot, which go to the founding of the *duomo,* or cathedral.
1075	Pisa develops its own code of laws, the *Consuetudini di mare.*
1081	Holy Roman Emperor Henry IV grants Pisa full independence as a commune. The Pisan republic is born.
1095	At Clermont, Pope Urban II preaches the First Crusade.
1099	Pisa participates in the First Crusade, and Cuccodei Ricucchi, a Pisan, is the first to scale the walls of Jerusalem.
	Pisan commerce thrives, and by the twelfth century, Pisa has consuls in Acre, Alexandria, Damietta, Armenia, Salerno, and Naples, and there are Pisan colonies in Antioch, Tripoli, Tyre, Jaffa, Bona, Bugia, and Tunis.
1111	Pisa concludes a treaty with Byzantium, gaining free transit for Pisan trade in the Holy Land.
1118	Pisan duomo consecrated by Pope Gelasius II.
1136	Pisa raids Amalfi.

1153	Work commenced on Pisan baptistery.
1172	The Pisan widow Berta di Bernardo leaves "sixty coins" in her will for the purchase of stone to build a bell tower, or campanile, for the cathedral.
1173	Construction of the Tower of Pisa begins.
1178	Work on the tower comes to a halt, with the structure standing just over three stories tall.
1228	Pisa defeats the united forces of Florence and Lucca.
1254	Florence defeats Pisa.
1260	Ghibelline Pisa participates in the rout of the Tuscan Guelphs at Montaperto.
1272	Work resumes on the campanile, directed by Giovanni di Simone.
1276	Pisa defeated by Guelph League and compelled to agree to harsh terms, including the exemption of Florentine merchandise from all harbor duties and the relinquishing of territory to Lucca.
1278	Construction of the campanile reaches the height of the seventh cornice, but work again comes to a halt.
1284	Genoa defeats Pisa at the Battle of Meloria. Chroniclers record five thousand Pisan dead, eleven thousand taken prisoner, and the loss of most of the Pisan fleet.

1293	Guelph forces enter the Pisan port, block it with sunken vessels, and seize the harbor towers. More harsh terms imposed on Pisa include the loss of Pisan territory on Corsica and Sardinia.
1298	First commission convened to investigate the Tower of Pisa's tilt.
1301	Andrea Orcagna paints his celebrated frescoes in the Camposanto.
1313	Uguccione della Faggiola is elected Pisan *podestà* and captain of the people, but his rule is so tyrannical that he is driven from the city in 1316.
1338	University of Pisa founded.
1370	The Tower of Pisa is officially completed; its inclination measures 1.6 degrees from vertical.
1406	Florence besieges Pisa by land and sea and takes the city in October.
1499–1505	Sieges by Florence.
1509	Urged on by Niccolò Machiavelli, the secretary of the Ten, Florence ravages Pisa. The city finally surrenders in June. Henceforth, the Florentines rule over Pisa.
1564	Galileo Galilei born in Pisa to Vincenzo Galilei, a musician, teacher, and occasional wool trader, and his wife, Giulia Ammannati.

1589–1591	Galileo lectures as a young professor of mathematics at the Pisa university. It is during this period that he is purported to have conducted experiments on falling objects, using the campanile as his laboratory.
1595	Duomo partially destroyed by fire.
1633	Galileo is found guilty of heresy by the Inquisition on the basis of his defense of the Copernican theory of the solar system published in 1632 in *The Dialogue Concerning the Two Chief World Systems*.
1787	Alessandro Da Morrona measures the tilt of the tower at "six and a half arms" (approximately 3.8 meters).
1817	Edward Cresy and George Ledwell Taylor, English architects and engravers, arrive in Pisa and proceed to systematically render the monuments of the Campo dei Miracoli. They also measure the tower's inclination at "12 feet, 7 inches" (3.84 meters).
1818	Percy Bysshe Shelley and his wife, Mary, arrive in Pisa, fleeing the social constraints of late-Georgian England. Lord Byron follows, along with some lesser lights of the period, and the "Pisa Circle" forms.
1822	Percy Bysshe Shelley and Edward Williams

There were plans from proper engineers, schoolchildren, inspired amateur inventors, and a wide assortment of crackpots. Some proposed that the tower be painstakingly dismantled and rebuilt, others that it be hoisted by hydraulic lifts, sheathed in scaffolding, encased in plastic, or strung upright with a web of steel cables. Then there was the offer by a Chinese architectural engineer named Cao Shizhong of the Slanting Building Correction Research Institute in Hangzhou. Mr. Cao, a fixer of skewed smokestacks and tipping pagodas, arrived in Pisa proclaiming that only Chinese technology could save the tower, but then adamantly refused to reveal his methods.

"Many of the proposals were clearly competent, but most of them failed to consider two factors," recalls Professor Burland. "First, on a strictly aesthetic level, the measures couldn't obscure the beauty of the tower, at least not in the long term, which effectively precluded the great majority of plans that called for some sort of structure built alongside the tower in order to prop it up. Second, few people realized just how precarious the tower was. Even approaching the structure with machinery or building materials would put it at risk of collapse. Whatever measure we would eventually adopt had to be extremely non-invasive."

Progress was excruciatingly slow due not only to the structural fragility Professor Burland describes, but also, in large part, to an Italian bureaucracy of almost sinister proportions. The Commission, born by decree, had never been

	drown while sailing in the Gulf of Spezia.
1838	The architect Alessandro della Gherardesca excavates a walkway, or *catino*, around the base of the tower. His intervention is a disaster, as it induces water to flood the base of the campanile and sets the tower in motion after centuries of stability.
1840	Second commission to investigate the tower convened.
1902	On July 14, at 9:47 A.M., the campanile in Venice's Piazza San Marco collapses.
1907–1908	Third commission convened.
1912	Fourth commission convened.
1924, 1925, 1926, 1927, 1932	A string of commissions address the campanile's state. Two are formed in 1926 alone.
1934	An ill-advised plan with Italian dictator Benito Mussolini's blessing drills 361 holes into the base of the campanile and injects ninety tons of cement in an attempt to stabilize it. The measure very nearly topples the tower.
1943–1945	The Allied Italian campaign of World War II. Although Pisa is heavily bombed,

the duomo, baptistery, and campanile emerge virtually unscathed. The Camposanto, however, is hit by an incendiary grenade, and frescoes and other treasures are lost.

1964, 1965, 1972, 1983, 1988	More commissions, but still no solutions.
1989	On March 17, the Civic Tower in Pavia falls, killing four.
1990	The Italian government closes the Tower of Pisa and convenes the seventeenth commission.
1995	On a summer night in a month remembered as "Black September" by commission members, the campanile nearly collapses in the midst of work to install stabilizing cables.
1999	Engineers begin the delicate process of soil extraction that will prove to be the definitive solution to the Tower of Pisa's stability.
2001	On June 16, Pisa celebrates the restoration of the tower.

TILT

ONE

Commissione #17

No one need worry that the tower is going to end up straight; that is one of two unacceptable results. The other we don't dare mention.

—John Burland, professor of soil mechanics, Imperial College, London, and a member of the seventeenth commission appointed to rescue the Tower of Pisa, 1990

O n March 17, 1989, the eleventh-century Civic Tower in Pavia, Italy, suddenly and unexpectedly collapsed, burying four passers-by beneath a jumble of Romanesque and Renaissance rubble. The disaster, due to structural failure, sent Italians into national mourning, both for the innocent victims, as well as for a venerable piece of architecture. The dust had scarcely settled in Pavia's Piazza Vittoria, however, before the public's attention came to focus intently and urgently on Pisa, as it tends to do when any significant edifice falls down in Italy.

Unlike the Civic Tower, which hadn't even been leaning, the Tower of Pisa has never known a correct perpendicular. Since construction began in 1173, this campanile of the cathedral of Santa Maria Maggiore has suffered from progressive degrees of inclination until, at the time of the Pavia tragedy, it was tilting to the south by a full 5.5 degrees. Put another way, the seventh and topmost cornice protruded over the first cornice by 4.5 meters, approximately 15 feet. Yet there it stands. For centuries, this fragile Romanesque bell tower, built of luminous white San Giuliano and Carrara marble, lime, and other assorted stones, has teetered on the brink of oblivion, but neither earthquakes, war, misguided architectural interventions, or even the relentless onslaught of contemporary tourism has ever managed to topple it—although some have come perilously close. That the tower still stands after more than eight hundred eventful years defies logic, gravity, and all the odds.

Not surprisingly, Pisan lore is full of tales that purport to explain the tilt of the city's beloved campanile (in Italian, *campanilismo* is also used as a term for local pride) to a host of intrigues both colorful and wholly groundless. The original laborers conspired to create the faulty perpendicular, it is sometimes said, to protest their meager wages. Others point to a curse by the Saracens or the bitter rival Genoese. Still another fanciful plot lays the blame squarely on one William of Innsbruck, a builder who is said to have collaborated with Bonnano Pisano, the campanile's disputed architect. William, it seems, deliberately built the tower askew to extract revenge on humanity for his own twisted infirmity: he was a hunchback. And then there is the pious explanation, which attributes the unbalanced phenomenon to the Divine: rising as the tower does in the so-called Campo dei Miracoli, or Field of Miracles, it is God who has pitched the structure and allowed it to stand, as a sign of His infinite power and glory. In fact, the truth is considerably more prosaic. The campanile is built on unstable subsoil made up of soft estuarine deposits of sandy and clayey silts laid down under tidal conditions tens of thousands of years ago. The Field of Miracles, it seems, was once a bog.

In the wake of the Pavia disaster, the issue of the Tower of Pisa's safety and stability sparked a heated national debate that promptly grew into a full-blown political crisis pitting preservationists against Pisan authorities and merchants. The former claimed that a fallen Tower of Pisa would be an inestimable loss of universal patrimony, and that intervention was a cultural imperative. No one, they insisted, was suggesting that the tower be brought to a correct perpendicular that it had never known—a righted tower would surely lose a palpable measure of pathos, if nothing else. What the structure needed was to be stabilized. To not act was to condemn the campanile to certain collapse and invite a human and artistic tragedy of untold dimensions. The latter, on the other hand, operated on an equally compelling, but rather less high-minded, premise. A Tower of Pisa closed for renovations for years on end and possibly even inadvertently knocked down in the process (or, worse still, righted!), they contended, would

Campo dei Miracoli, 1909

crush Pisa economically. They weren't without a certain rationale, however self-serving: the lion's share of the city's revenues derive from the tourist trade, and what the tourists come to see is the Leaning Tower of Pisa, the wonder of the world, the architectural icon, the stuff of which enigmas are made. Never mind that the tower is only one of the buildings (and arguably the least captivating in purely aesthetic terms) in the Campo dei Miracoli, which also includes the *duomo,* or cathedral, of Santa Maria Maggiore, a baptistery, and the Camposanto cemetery—what the droves want to find suspended in the clear Tuscan air is logic. Without a tilting campanile, Pisa would fall off the map, and the locals know it. It is no small irony that the

Tower of Pisa, built as a symbol of the wealth and power of a medieval maritime republic, has become the very commodity on which the local economy depends.

In the absence of a consensus in the Italian parliament to intervene in the matter of the state of the tower, Prime Minister Giulio Andreotti exercised his right of decree and, on December 6, 1989, he ordered the campanile to be closed and an international commission to be formed, with a mandate to stabilize and safeguard the tower. The Pisan shopkeepers protested, but the evidence in favor of interceding was overwhelming. The tower's tilt stood at a precarious 5.5 degrees, that is to say, 4.5 meters out of plumb, top to ground, a figure that was growing at a rate of one millimeter per year. To a layman that might be a hair-breadth, but to an engineer it's a number that inspires alarm. The least disturbance—a tremor, a moderate storm, a fluctuation in the water table, an overabundance of tourists, or even a sudden change of temperature—could have caused the campanile to come crashing down. The tower's condition could be described only as terminal, and unless a solution to ensure its stability could be found, the tower would be doomed and with it much of Pisa's life's blood, namely, its tourist revenue.

The announcement of the formation of an international commission to save their campanile was something that Pisans had heard before, and the news was greeted with a certain timeworn cynicism. Over the centuries, no less than sixteen committees or commissions had been given the very same task; the first, in 1298, was presided over by the sculptor and architect Giovanni Pisano, and it stirred up considerable public interest. When it came time to measure the tower's imperfection, Giovanni's experiments and calculations were carried out before a throng and under the scrupulous gaze of a notary public. At that time, the tower was already 1 degree, or about 1.4 meters, off perpendicular, according to Giovanni, but with work already completed up to the seventh and final cornice, little could be done to correct the flaw. For more than five hundred years, the subject was considered all but closed. The next commission did not convene until 1840, by which time the Tower of Pisa, already a renowned architectural oddity, was tilting more than four meters. The remaining fourteen commissions worked throughout the twentieth century, each, regrettably, as ineffectual as the last. Pisans simply couldn't believe that the seventeenth commission would be any different. Who could blame them?

On a March morning in 1990, a full year after the collapse of the Civic Tower in Pavia, John Burland, professor of soil mechanics at London's Imperial College of Science, Technology, and Medicine, received a telephone call from Michele Jamiolkowski, a friend and fellow engineer, in Milan. The crux of the conversation, recalls Professor Burland, went something like this:

"Good morning, John, it's Michele. You won't believe what I've just discovered. There's a piece in today's newspaper about a plan to save the Tower of Pisa. Andreotti has set up a commission, and it seems that I am to be the chairman."

"Oh, Michele, I'm so sorry. You know what a poison chalice that tower has always been."

"Save your sympathy. Among the other names on the list is a certain *professore* John Burland!"

The choice of John Burland was a wise one. The root of the Tower of Pisa's problem has always been shifting subsoil, and if there ever was a man or woman who knew dirt, it was Burland. He has made a career of studying the mechanical behavior of materials such as soil, clay, and rocks and applying his understanding to the design and construction of engineering projects. Among the other fourteen members of the Commission there were structural engineers, architects, restoration specialists, and, of course, a politician, but Burland was the only member, with the exception of Michele Jamiolkowski, also a geotechnical engineer, who could discover what was going on beneath the tower, where the structure's salvation lay. Burland also knew a thing or two about towers; it was he who propped up London's Big Ben clock tower while the Jubilee Underground line was being built. He has also stabilized a sinking foundation at the Metropolitan Cathedral in Mexico City and ameliorated devastating landslides in Hong Kong. And so he may well have regarded it, objectively, as a "poison chalice," but the cause of Pisa's campanile also captured his professional curiosity. "Saving the tower," he said, "would be the last great civil engineering challenge of the century and the millennium."

Structurally, the Tower of Pisa is rather less substantial than it appears. It consists of a hollow masonry cylinder surrounded by six uniform loggias, with the bell chamber at the top. The cylinder is formed not by solid marble blocks, but by two concentric marble walls filled with mortar and assorted rubble. A 293-step spiral staircase winds around the inner cylinder and leads to the arcaded stories and summit belfry. On the outside of the tower, the marble façade is rarely more than twenty-five centimeters thick. The whole structure is 60 meters tall and weighs 14,453 metric tons, but the 3-meter-deep foundation is wholly

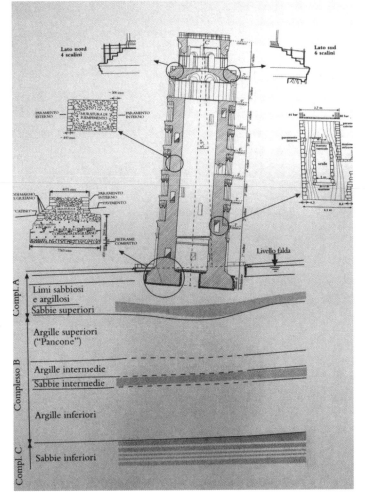

Works in progress to lower the inclination of the tower, 2000

inadequate for such a load. Whoever built the campanile, and the matter is a subject of perennial debate in Pisan circles, did so with calculations that were wildly off the mark.

It did not take long for Burland and his colleagues to realize that the state of the campanile was worse than anyone had suspected. As it happened, the risk to the tower was twofold: The stress and weight on the masonry could lead to structural failure, and the campanile would simply collapse as did the Civic Tower in Pavia or the bell tower in the Piazza San Marco in Venice in 1902. Alternatively, the subsoil around the foundation could break up or otherwise shift, and the campanile would duly tip over, which is just how most of us have always imagined that the Tower of Pisa would one day be done in. Either way, the prospects looked grim.

Eight hundred years and the elements had clearly taken their toll. Although a great deal of the tower's original San Giuliano marble—including 175 of its 269 columns and 195 of the 207 capitols—had been replaced over the centuries with more durable Carrara marble, all of the campanile's stone was suffering from various degrees of crumbling, disintegration, pulverization, and a blight known as black crust. The principal threats to the stone came from rain, particle deposits, and abrupt changes in temperature. Furthermore, in the area beneath the actual inclination, whole sections showed signs of compression and there were cracks and fissures running through much of the stone, particularly at the levels of the first and second orders, where the stress was most acute. If the tower were to buckle and fall, this is where the failure in the masonry would occur—specifically, they found, at the point on the second floor where a doorway meets the staircase.

In order to gain time to gather data, conduct tests and trials, and devise definitive stabilization measures, the Commission approved a number of temporary interventions. First, plastic-coated steel tendons were wrapped around the tower's girth at the height of the second-story gallery; this relieved the stress on the tower's weakest structural point and helped to close cracks and cavities. Next, workers poured a temporary concrete ring around the base of the tower, to provide a foundation on which to lay down a series of specially cast lead ingots—each weighing hundreds of tons—on the campanile's north side. These measures were unsightly and, given the accumulated scientific expertise of the Commission members, singularly crude. But they were also undeniably effective, as the tower soon tilted back to the north, or vertical, by fifty-two arc seconds. For the first time in centuries, scientists had won back a fraction of the inevitable. Still, it was little more than a brief reprieve.

What the Commission needed was data, and considerably more than could be provided by a 1934-vintage pendulum and spirit level, the last monitoring devices to have been installed in the tower. By 1991, the campanile was wired with sensors to measure exterior wind, air temperature, solar radiation, seismic activity, horizontal-point movement, dimensional variation in vertical and horizontal sections, width of fissures, and masonry temperature in the structure itself, not to mention levels within the strata underlying the tower. The Tower of Pisa had become, by all accounts, the most relentlessly monitored edifice in the world. Among other details, sensors revealed that every day, due to changes in temperature, the entire tower sways in a minute circle not more than one hundredth of an inch in diameter. As the sun heats the south side of the tower more than the north, the marble there expands, disturbing the equilibrium and increasing the tilt. At night, as the temperature falls, the tower retreats, gently completing the day's sway. The structure was also shown to be highly sensitive to changes in the level of the water table, to gusts of wind during summer storms, and to freezing rain in the winter. In a region notorious for its seismic activity, it was further calculated that the tower would unlikely withstand any earthquake in excess of grade VI on the Mercalli scale that measures the intensity of earthquakes. As for inclination, the tower remained relatively steady at 5.5 degrees—but when technicians created a precise computer model of the structure, they couldn't get it to remain standing at that angle. At 5.44 degrees, the model teetered and collapsed. All of this measurement and data starkly illustrated just how delicate the 818-year-old campanile really was.

Meanwhile, the tower was fast becoming a sort of preservation and engineering cause célèbre, and proposals to save the campanile were flooding in from all parts.

ratified by the Italian parliament. Italian law, however, stipulates that a decree must be ratified by the parliament within two months of its publication in the *Gazzetta Ufficiale* or else it becomes invalid. Consequently, every two months, the Commission's decree had to be renewed— although sometimes it wasn't, on account of some political machination or another, and work had to be abruptly suspended. All the while, the media was hounding Commission members, and before too long coverage of the Commission's efforts and the whole rescue project began to take on an increasingly mocking tone. Pisan merchants continued to mutter about the loss of revenues on account of the campanile's closure, while interference from the local authorities, numerous changes of government, strikes, incessant criticism from every side, and the inevitable jealousies and backbiting within the Commission itself all took a toll. Burland's poison chalice had begun to seem an appropriate metaphor.

Still, work continued. In September 1995, engineers began installing a series of underground cables that would be anchored in bedrock forty meters beneath the surface, a system intended to replace the unsightly, cyclopean lead ingots that had been piled on the north side of the tower's foundation for more than two years. The pull of the anchors on the tower's foundation was to replace the push of the lead ingots. As contractors drilled into the soft soil, liquid nitrogen, at $-200°F$, was injected into the ground to freeze the surrounding water and prevent it from flooding the operation. The procedure began and went according to plan, at least on the tower's north side. When the drilling reached the sensitive south side of the tower, however, monitors began to pick up movement. Then, at 3:30 A.M. on September 6, the top of the campanile suddenly pitched four millimeters to the south. Workers rushed to pile more massive lead ingots on the tower's foundation to halt the movement. In one terrifying night that Commission members would come to remember as Black September, the tower lurched more in an instant than it ordinarily did in a year.

For months after the incidents of Black September, work in the Campo dei Miracoli came to a virtual standstill. There was a feeling among the Commission members, technicians, and laborers that they had fallen prey to the centuries-old irony that has plagued the campanile: it is in the name of saving the tower, after all, that man has come closest to destroying it. No one dared suggest how to proceed. Perhaps there was no solution to the campanile's tilted fate, and the Pisan merchants had been right. Then came a bombshell from Rome: in late 1996, Commissione #17 was summarily and unceremoniously disbanded. Six years of research, studies, analysis, trials, small victories, and a glaring defeat were lost, and the campanile stood more poised than ever for collapse. As it turns out, disaster wan't far off or long in coming.

On September 26, 1997, a devastating earthquake measuring 6.0 on the Richter scale struck the area around

Assisi, Umbria, the venerated birthplace of St. Francis, a mere two hundred kilometers south of Pisa. The disaster left nine dead, including two Franciscan friars, and forty thousand homeless, and caused an incalculable sum in damages to scores of historic buildings, monuments, and works of art. At the thirteenth-century Basilica di San Francesco, Giotto's exquisite frescoes depicting the life of the saint, as well as other frescoes by Giotto's teacher, Giovanni Cimabue, and Pietro Cavallini, were severely damaged. Were an equally destructive earthquake to strike Pisa, experts claimed, there was little doubt that the tower would crumble.

In Parliament, there was much finger pointing, widespread evasion of responsibilities, some high-minded talk on the virtues of preservation, and new legislation earmarking billions of lire for the conservation of the nation's artistic patrimony, the Tower of Pisa included. Ironically, it was precisely the same reaction as that which had followed the Pavia disaster eight years before. Within weeks, Commissione #17 reconvened in Pisa.

So there they were again, some of the greatest engineering minds of our day, gathered in the Campo dei Miracoli and staring up at a tower which had appealed to their vanity, tested their expertise, tried their patience, frayed their nerves, caused them undeserved humiliation, and sent them away cursing. The same tower that, despite it all, they still wanted so desperately to save. For all their research, and data, and high-tech instruments, and cumulative wisdom, however, the Tower of Pisa still remained an enigma, an eight-hundred-year-old mystery from its *catino* to its belfry. It wasn't just that the campanile had a persistent habit of acting unpredictably, scorning well-intentioned efforts, or defying the statistics. It was the whole idea of the thing: anyone hoping to solve the puzzle of the tower had to go way back to its very inception, or even before that, to the threshold of the second millennium, and ask why these upstart Pisans had chosen to build such a grandiose and ambitious campanile atop so inadequate a foundation in the midst of such soggy and shifting terrain? And why, unlike all the other structures which grace the Campo dei Miracoli, had no architect chosen to sign the tower? Was it simply the first premonition that nothing with this audacious campanile would ever be quite straight?

TWO

Afloat on a
Blood-Red Sea

The Mediterranean, which had, in a sense, been growing
stagnant after the collapse of the western Roman Empire,
had been stirred up by a gale from the East. When the
storm subsided and the sand-fevered sea put on its blue
again, it would be seen that many previously familiar
landmarks had gone for ever. Cities and cultures that had
withstood the mute erosion of time were transformed by
the great Arab invasions.

—Ernle Bradford, *Mediterranean: Portrait of a Sea* (1971)

In the closing centuries of the first millennium, the
Tyrrhenian Sea, that stretch of the western Mediterranean
between the Italian peninsula and the islands of Corsica, Sardinia, and Sicily, was as lawless and sanguinary a body of water as medieval chroniclers could fathom, and Pisa lay
strategically on its shore, scant miles inland from the mouth
of the Arno River. Long gone were the imperial days when
Italy's coast and islands were protected by Rome's Praetorian

fleet sailing out of Misenum on the Bay of Naples and a prosperous Pisa, then known as Colonia Julia Pisana, enjoyed the patronage of the family of the emperor Augustus. With the death throes and final fall of imperial Rome in the fifth and sixth centuries came a succession of raiders, pirates, and plunderers of varying degrees of ferocity and greed: Vandals, Byzantine Greeks, even Vikings, periodically sacked Pisa, slaughtered locals or took them as slaves, and attacked and looted the city's commercial ships. Under the nominal feudal rule of a distant, indifferent lord, the marquise of Tuscany, the city was, in essence, defenseless. The only measure of solace for the Pisans was that none of the marauders seemed inclined to stay. It was piracy, not invasion.

By the eighth century, however, a new protagonist appeared on the western sea. He was no barbarian or near-barbarian, nor was he a pagan—but he was not a Christian either. This was a wholly new foe, risen from the worldly East, fired by a newly begotten, uncorrupted faith, and devoted to its spread and dominion; he was the Muslim, or, perhaps more commonly but less properly, the Mohammedan, the Saracen, or the Moor, and he orchestrated an invasion that would transform the Mediterranean world forever, and with it, the fate of Pisa.

It took the Saracens,* as they were known through

*The Saracens, properly, are a tribe hailing from the region of modern Syria and Jordan. The term was adapted throughout Europe in the Middle Ages to refer to all Arabs and, more generally, Muslims. The author uses the term in the broader sense and without malice.

much of Europe, less than a century from the death of the prophet Mohammed in A.D. 632 to rise up like a desert wind from the Arabian peninsula and sweep across Persia to the east and in the west the Levant, Asia Minor, Egypt, and North Africa to the Pillars of Hercules and Iberia, and so to Europe. By any measure it was an astonishing progress, but it likely would never have occurred, and certainly would never have offered any degree of permanency, had not the Arabs, natural horsemen, come to master the sea, or, to be more precise, to conquer lands and bring under their domain seafaring peoples and cultures. The Arabs held little affinity and a good measure of suspicion toward the sea, notwithstanding the thriving maritime traditions of the Red Sea. When it was suggested to Amr, Muslim conqueror of Alexandria, for example, that he commission a fleet to extend his realm, his response was indicative of the desert dweller's aversion to the nautical world: "If a ship lies still, it rends the heart; if it moves it terrifies the imagination. Upon it a man's power ever diminishes and calamity increases. Those within it are like worms in a log, and if it rolls over they are drowned."

Hence, much as the Romans had benefited from the maritime prowess of the Greeks, so too the Arabs developed a fleet by proxy. The Muslim forces first drew their fleet and the sailors to man it from the ports and fishing villages of Phoenicia, and later from Syria and Egypt. These ancient maritime cultures provided a force of Tyrian, Tripolitan, and Alexandrian navigators and traders who in turn made an incalculable contribution to the rapid spread of Islamic culture, faith, and rule. Only when the Arabs took to the sea, in fact, did they finally come to present a true threat not merely to the Mediterranean, but to the whole of Europe.

Islamic forces captured much of Iberia—al-Andalus, they called it—in the early eighth century. From there and points across North Africa, they began to explore the European Mediterranean and Italy's western coast. Initially, the Saracens confined their activities to periodic incursions along the Italian coast and throughout the islands in search of fast loot and highly profitable slaves to be sold in the markets of Alexandria, Cairo, Damascus, and Baghdad. Soon enough, however, the newcomers began to search out a permanent base as well as a gateway to Europe, and they found it, as so many others had before them, in Sicily, then a possession of Byzantium—the Eastern Roman Empire. What the Saracens probably never imagined was that they would be invited in.

The Islamic conquest of Sicily began with an act of treason. Euphemius of Syracuse, a mutinous Greek general seeking to carve out his own sovereign turf, appealed for the aid of Prince Ziyadet Allah of the North African Aghlabid dynasty. The Muslim forces, comprising Arabs, Berbers, Spanish Moors, and Sudanese, sailed from Sousse in Tunisia and landed on Sicily's southern coast in 827. With this invasion Sicily became

Italy, 1521

yet again the bloodstained battleground that it had been for Greeks and Carthaginians, and later for Carthaginians and Romans. By 832, the invaders had taken much of the island, including Palermo, which they made their capital and the seat of the emir, or lord; eleven years later Messina capitulated. Thereafter, not only was the bridgehead to the Italian mainland open, but by patrolling the narrow stretch between western Sicily and Tunis, the Saracen fleets could control access to the whole of the western Mediterranean. (More than a thousand years later, the same strategy would be used by the Allies in the Italian campaign of World War II.) It did not take long for the Saracen forces to overrun Calabria and Apulia and seize Bari. In 846, Rome itself was put to siege; the Vicar of Christ, Sergius II, an ineffectual and gout-ridden pontiff, was made to pay a humiliating tribute, and, for good measure, the churches of St. Peter and St. Paul were stripped of their considerable riches and finery. And although the Arabs never held their mainland conquests for long, as Sicily, Corsica, Sardinia, and the Balearic Islands successively fell to Islamic armies, the waters of the western Mediterranean seemed increasingly like a Muslim lake. In the eastern sea, especially in the Aegean, the fleets of Byzantium still maintained a tenuous control, but elsewhere, from the Levant to Cadiz, the Muslims were achieving a disturbing hegemony, and Christianity itself seemed to hang precariously in the balance.

Pisa, of course, was neither immune nor idle. Already, in 828, a Pisan fleet under the command of Bonifacio de Lucca, marquis of Tuscany, had defeated the naval forces of the emir Mohammed ibn al-Gawari in five assaults along the North African coast. The campaign was significant not only on account of the Christian victory in distant waters, but also because it showed Pisa capable of building and maintaining a worthy fleet. The Romans had used Pisa as a shipbuilding center, drawn by the quality of the area timber and the protection and convenience afforded by the Arno River. That Pisa was capable of mustering a home fleet centuries later proved that the city's maritime tradition was alive and well. It was the Saracens, however, who provided the Pisans with the impetus to grow strong, and to expand their influence and do battle to protect their commercial interests.

The Pisans were not raiders and plunderers, but traders, blessed with a natural penchant for commerce, what is known in the Mediterranean world as a "Carthaginian spirit." Even during the desperate years of the barbarian invasions and the centuries of instability that followed, Pisa distinguished itself from other Tuscan towns in her reliance on the sea and the communications she maintained with the coastal fringes of the former Roman Empire. The Pisans were not driven so much by empire or religion as by commerce; the city wanted ports of call for her commercial fleet and marketplaces where her merchants could trade. Much has been made, especially by medieval chroniclers, of the spirit of the anti-Saracen campaigns undertaken by Pisa and Genoa, Venice, and, to a lesser extent, Amalfi, Italy's other maritime states; some go so far as to characterize the conflict as a kind of trial run for the Crusades. Yet religious sentiment seems to have had rather little to do with Pisa's, or the other states', desire to stem the Islamic invasion. Indeed, a whole procession of popes, starting with Leo IV in 848, had been exhorting Italian cities and feudal lords alike to rise up against the infidels and in defense of the Cross, but to little widespread enthusiasm. Moreover, with Christianity itself split between Rome and Byzantium, the message was muddled at best. Promises of sure and speedy salvation, the forgiveness of sins (*peccaminum remissio*) and a new path to heaven (*novum salutis genus*), were lofty enough, but the Pisans were concerned with more worldly matters: it was not the defense of the faith that consumed them, but the fate of their markets, their galleys, their sailors, and their cargoes, more or less in that order.

Throughout the ninth and tenth centuries, the Saracens increasingly threatened Pisa's natural trade routes throughout the western sea, and there were constant skirmishes between the ships of the rival forces. Then, in 1004, the Saracens attacked Pisa itself, razing a good bit of it in the process, and taking many townspeople as slaves. Thereafter, the Pisans seem to have decided that enough was enough. A sustained counteroffensive may have been long overdue, but once Pisa decided upon a concerted military response, her forces and fleet took to their new, aggressive role exceedingly well. In 1011, the Pisans turned back another Saracen attack, and in the first half of the eleventh century, Pisa scored victories against the Saracens in Calabria, Sardinia, Corsica, North Africa, and on the high seas. Only Sicily, now the center of Saracen power in the Tyrrhenian Sea and the site of a flourishing civilization, remained too formidable a foe for the Pisans to take on alone. With each victory, however, Pisa was growing stronger and accumulating substantial treasure—by plunder and ransom alike—commercial advantages, and prestige. In a good many western Mediterranean ports, the Pisan standard, a red cross on a white field, flew as a beacon of safe conduct and passage for Christian merchants and marine traffic. The Pisans, meanwhile, were being heralded, as were the Genoese and the Venetians, as the deliverers of Christendom, and no one doubted their right to grow immeasurably rich in the process. Not coincidentally, the dawn of the second millennium was also the dawn of the Italian maritime republics, those upstart city-states that would cast off their feudal trammels and turn the swollen Saracen tide.

Without sea power, of course, Pisa was nothing. As Michele Amari, the nineteenth-century Italian orientalist and historian, and author of *The History of the Muslims in Sicily,* says of the city in this era, "the Pisans were already independent by sea, while still enslaved on land." Popes and emperors and local lords all asserted various formal claims on Pisa's allegiances. In practice, however, the city was independent, economically self-sufficient, and administratively autonomous, and, furthermore, she could defend those interests with seaborne military and commercial prowess. The development of a fleet as a means to extend the power, commerce, and influence of a state was an ancient principle; Themistocles had urged the same upon Athens in order to transform that modest state into a great one. The example was followed in turn by Rhodes, Carthage, Rome, Byzantium, the Saracens, and finally the Italian maritime republics. Pisa never called for a liberator or protector during this period; when it came time to do battle, the city rallied her own fleet and defended herself on what she had long considered to be her sea.

The true source of Pisa's wealth and her most cherished asset was, understandably, her galleys. These ships that carried Pisan trade and took on the Saracens did not differ radically from the classical bireme of the Greeks or the liburna of the Roman imperial fleet: they were long, single-banked vessels, approximately 150 feet in length, propelled principally by the bent backs and tempered arms of more than a hundred oarsmen, but also equipped with sails for traversing the open sea. Crews, numbering between 175 and 200 men, consisted of officers, who were usually of noble birth; marines, soldiers assigned to protect the ships as well as to keep crews in line; sailors; and oarsmen. For obvious reasons, a galley could only sustain high speeds in short bursts while under oar, but given a fair

The Taking of Damietta by Saint Louis IX, by Vincent de Beauvais, 1249

wind in addition to muscle, the vessels could attain speeds well in excess of ten knots.

Such vessels were well suited for trade on the Mediterranean, but, of necessity, had also to be outfitted and deployed for war. At this, too, the Pisans proved adept in the sporadic encounters they found. In battle, as in ancient times, the war galley's most formidable weapon was the ram, which was supplemented by flights of arrows loosed by marines and sailors. Tactics too differed little from a millennium past: the object was for rival ships to interlock and allow the crews to engage in arm-to-arm combat. "Greek fire," a precursor of napalm that was invented by the Byzantines, was also used to terrifying effect, as described in this account of a confrontation between Pisan ships and a Byzantine fleet: the ships "had at their prow the head of a lion or other land animal, made of brass or iron, with the mouth open, and all gilded so that the very aspect was terrifying. The fire which he directed against the enemy was passed through tubes set in the mouths of these beasts, so that it seemed as if the lions and other monsters were vomiting fire." Further, in addition to their ships and seamanship, the Pisans enjoyed one more crucial advantage over their Saracen enemies—their galleys were manned by freemen, as opposed to the slaves who habitually took the oars in the Muslim fleets. Accordingly, the Pisans fought with greater conviction. They also made a habit of promptly freeing any slaves who came into their custody. By the middle of the eleventh century, the Saracens maintained their bastion in Sicily, but nearly everywhere else throughout the western Mediterranean, the Muslim forces were in irreversible retreat.

It would take the ambition of the Normans, the new arrival in Italy and on the western sea, to invade and begin the reconquest of Sicily. Curiously enough, just as the Muslim invasion of the island had been instigated by treason, so too was that of the Normans. This time, the traitor was Becumen of Catania, an exiled Muslim lord who urged the Norman Count Roger of Hauteville to invade Sicily and establish a Latin kingdom. Taking the offer, Roger seized Messina in 1060 and there established a temporary Norman capital, so beginning a slow but sure battle of reconquest that would consume the island for thirty years. Interestingly, the reception offered Roger and his Norman knights was not always welcoming, for while in many places the local Christians hailed the conqueror, in others the Saracens were well established and, frankly, well liked. At Troina, for example, the locals joined the Saracen forces to attack Roger's position in the citadel, from which the count only narrowly escaped.

The Sicilian ambivalence toward their Christian "saviors" is perhaps understandable, considering the autocratic rule and excessive taxation exacted by the island's former Byzantine rulers. Under the Saracens, Sicily, although often fractured by internal feuds, had prospered and become the center of a brilliant Islamic civilization that excelled in architecture, literature, and the sciences.

Palermo, which contemporary accounts describe as a city of three hundred thousand inhabitants and three hundred mosques, was considered one of the great capitals of the civilized world, surpassed only by Baghdad, Constantinople, and Cordoba. Moreover, agriculture was bolstered with a fine irrigation system, some of which is still in evidence today, and Sicily came to be known as a garden paradise. Commerce also flourished, as the island's geographic position made it a crossroads in a vast Muslim sphere stretching from Syria to Spain. Sicilian life, in short, wasn't so bad under the Saracens. "Once established, the new masters of the country were fairly easy-going," wrote Denis Mack Smith in *Medieval Sicily* (1968). "Some towns were left virtually independent with not even a garrison. The new regime may well have seemed less oppressive than were the Christian Lombards or Franks on the mainland, and less religiously intolerant than the iconoclastic Church at Constantinople. Local institutions were often retained, and though many churches became mosques, in general Christians could live by their own laws, with the same legal guarantee of person and property as Moslems." Once the Normans invaded, however, Muslim Sicily was doomed. Some Saracen enclaves would hold out and resist the Christian forces for decades, but the island would never again be a Muslim domain.

As it happened, the Norman invasion proved a boon for Pisa; a Sicily under siege and divided was precisely what the Pisans had been waiting for. With much of the Saracen forces engaged against the Normans in the northeast of the island, the Pisans saw their chance to strike Muslim Sicily at its heart. In 1063, the Pisan fleet made an audacious assault on the port of Palermo, the Muslim capital and very jewel in the Sicilian crown. In a campaign of widespread looting and destruction, relates Michele Amari, five Saracen ships were sunk in the harbor, while another was filled with treasure and towed back to Pisa. Wisely, the Pisans left the complete conquest of Sicily to the Normans, but in taking advantage of their own opportunity inadvertently afforded by the Normans, they freed their trade routes of the Saracen threat, and their fleet could now ply the western sea virtually unchallenged. As for that shipload of treasure towed back from Palermo, the booty was requisitioned for the building of a cathedral that would forever be the symbol of Pisa and Christendom triumphant.

THREE

Booty Transformed

"The two intellectual powers of Architecture are veneration and dominion."

—John Ruskin, *The Seven Lamps of Architecture* (1849)

The Pisa to which the victorious fleet returned in 1063 was altogether less glorious than the Palermo which its forces had only just ravaged. The city had been a Roman colony, true enough, even a prosperous one, but it was no Pompeii, Verona, Orange, or even Timgad. Gaius and Lucius, grandsons of Augustus, had been patrons of Pisa; and after their death, monuments were erected in their honor, but they have disappeared like so much else, the victims of pillage or neglect. Indeed, all that remains today of the Roman epoch in Pisa are the ruins of some baths built by Hadrian (erroneously attributed to Nero), a smattering of columns from the third century A.D., the skeleton of a temple precinct, and possibly a naval circus. There has been much speculation as to the existence of a forum or an amphitheater beneath the Piazza dei Cavalieri, but the site was chosen by the Medici in the sixteenth century for a cluster of palaces and a church by Giorgio Vasari, and no one has suggested disturbing Renaissance gems in the hope of uncovering hoary Roman ruins. From what historians and archaeologists can gather, eleventh-century Pisa, then located entirely on the right bank of the Arno and far nearer the sea than today, was a city built of mud brick, timber, and a good bit of recycled Roman stone (another reason for the scarcity of remains). Whatever splendor the city may have possessed had already suffered the wrath and torch of Vandals, Vikings, and Saracens. The city, in short, lacked an architectural landscape proportionate to its newfound station.

In Roman times, an emperor might have commissioned the building of a triumphal arch, but this was the Middle Ages, and in southern Europe especially, Christians and Muslims were competing for both spiritual and temporal powers. Any Pisan monument, then, would be a church; a place of worship, to be sure, but also a powerful symbol of Christendom triumphant and Pisa emergent. Hence, the spoils-laden galley won at Palermo was promptly requisitioned for the building of a great duomo, a cathedral to eclipse not only the magnificent churches of Rome and Constantinople but even the mosques of Cairo, Damascus, and Cordoba. That the foundation of the sacred was being laid with the fruits of war against the infidel was inherently proper to the medieval mind.

The site chosen for the cathedral lay outside Pisa's early medieval walls, in an area that had been sacred to the Etruscans, the pre-Roman inhabitants of the region. Nearby stood the remains of a Roman palace complex, possibly that of Hadrian; a Lombard cemetery; and an early Christian church dedicated to Santa Reparata, a third-century martyr beheaded during the reign of Decius for refusing to sacrifice to the pagan gods. The terrain was flat, open, of age-old religious significance, and, alas, prone to flooding. Above all, however, there was space, a scarcity in the cramped and crowded environs encompassed by the city walls.

The architect tapped by the archbishop and city fathers to create their duomo was Buscheto di Giovanni Guidice, likely a Tuscan, possibly even a Pisan, who had already distinguished himself with a number of local churches, including San Paolo a Ripa d'Arno, the architectural inspiration for the envisioned cathedral. Unlike the largely anonymous architects and master builders of those times, Buscheto, or at least his kin, saw to it that his name and reputation would achieve long renown, if not actual immortality. His sepulchre is not only set in a blind arcade of the cathedral façade—a place more apt for princes and bishops—but also bears the following glowing epitaph:

> Here lies Buscheto, whose genius exceeded that of King Ulysses, who, for all his sagacity, caused the ruin of the walls of Troy, while here the walls have been built due to the talent of a man. The one used his genius to destroy, the other used his genius to build. And your dark house, Daedalus, the labyrinth,

may be worthy of praise, but what splendid works
dignify Buscheto. The white marble temple built by
the genius Buscheto is without equal.

It was no mere hyperbole. Buscheto, the better of Ulysses
and Daedalus, had indeed built a temple that was,
arguably, without equal.

Buscheto lived and created his buildings during a time
of architectural transition. Monumental churches such as
the old St. Peter's or Santa Maria Maggiore in Rome, St.
Apollinaire in Ravenna, Charlemagne's Palatine Chapel
in Aachen, or even Justinian's great churches in Byzantium, such as the Hagia Sophia, were, for all their splendor and significance, by the eleventh century already
centuries old and architecturally dated. By the turn of
the first millennium, early Christian, Carolingian, and
Byzantine architectural models had grown stagnant and
repetitive. Even Venice's San Marco, begun in 1063—
coincidentally, the same year as the Pisa cathedral—while
most certainly an ambitious piece of architecture, was
hardly original: but for some minor alterations, it was an
unabashed copy of another of Justinian's churches in Constantinople, that of the Holy Apostles, dating from 536.
What emerged in Buscheto's time, in the interval between
the Byzantine era and the Gothic explosion of the twelfth
and thirteenth centuries, has gone by many names: it is
known as Lombard in Italy, Rhenish in Germany, Norman in France, and Saxon and Norman in England. In

the nineteenth century, however, French archaeologists and architectural historians adopted a generic catchall term, "Romanesque," to refer to the myriad forms and phases and geographical locations of this round-arched Christian style. Exactly what Buscheto would have called it is hard to say—"modern," most likely—and while it was new, there was little in it that was truly revolutionary. The Romanesque style took its share of cues from ancient Rome, but its power and widespread appeal lay in its ability to assimilate Roman architectural schemes with Byzantine, Lombard, and Islamic elements to create a

Cathedral at Pisa, Piazza del Duomo, circa 1200

style that physically manifested the diverse social and historical forces at play in the Mediterranean world at the start of the second millennium. To use a contemporary catchword, the Romanesque style was, above all, eminently multicultural.

Buscheto's vision for his site outside the city walls was as ambitious as Pisa's wildest maritime and mercantile dreams. The cathedral is Latin cross* in plan with double vaulted aisles on either side of the nave extending to the east and transepts with single aisles which end in apses. At the intersection of nave and transepts there is an elliptical dome of later design. A maze of second-story galleries called *matronei,* formerly the reserve of women, extend the length of the nave and the side aisles. There is a deep choir and a radiant clerestory. The whole interior scheme, with its exceptionally bold nave, side aisles, apses, towering colonnades, and clerestory, recalls the ancient Roman basilicas, or public halls, which, in turn, were the models and oftentimes the very foundations and walls for the early Christian basilicas. The resurrection of the style was especially pronounced in Tuscany, where ancient Roman architectural ideals were still not entirely extinguished, but there were other motives too, none aesthetic. During the eleventh and twelfth centuries, the Church was immersed

---

*One long arm (nave) and three shorter ones (apses and transepts). The Greek cross plan used in the Hagia Sophia, for example, is formed by four arms of more or less equal length.

NICHOLAS SHRADY

in an overdue process of *renovatio,* or renewal, which, along with other precepts, encouraged a return to purer roots and a more resolutely Christian faith before papal scandals; clerical debauchery; and the relentless threats of heresy, iconoclasm, and schism. Religious orders were reformed, the liturgy was purified, and architectural tastes settled on the basilica style as a means of emulating the exemplary early Christians. The model of the basilica had the ability to inspire equal measures of dignity and authority, and once stripped of its distant pagan associations, was used by church architects to great effect. In the tribune, where emperor and judges once sat in judgment and deliberation, the bishop and his clerical circle were now firmly ensconced.

Buscheto looked to Rome for inspiration, but he gave the cathedral a scale that would have humbled most emperors and their court architects. The Pisan duomo is, all other aesthetic concerns aside, positively massive, and the effect of such profound spatial richness on the Pisans and travelers of the day must have been overwhelming, as it still is for contemporary observers. The nave measures 320 feet in length, a good deal more than those of what were then the most emblematic churches in Christendom, the old St. Peter's (275 feet) and the Hagia Sophia (260 feet). The nave arcade is borne by monolithic columns and Corinthian capitals of the exquisite, pink-hued Elba marble; those of the side aisles are the spoils of ancient Greek and Roman buildings brought back by the Pisan galleys mostly from Sicily and Sardinia.* In addition to the common sense of recycling abundant building material of the finest quality, the use of ancient stone on such a colossal scale was a clear attempt to recapture the grandeur of an age that was lost forever, but hardly forgotten, even though the object of the glory and adoration was now a Christian god, rather than a pagan deity or a vainglorious Caesar.

Externally, the great volumes of the Latin cross extend to all the four points of the compass with the dome rising at the central axis. Aesthetically, the cathedral is one of the most sublime examples of Romanesque architecture; its rare degree of stylistic uniformity suggests that Buscheto designed the entire edifice of a piece, with the exception of the dome, an unfortunate fourteenth-century addition which displays a marked influence of the domed churches of Byzantium and the mosques of Sicily. The blind arcade of the ground story and the open galleries on the upper stories correspond to the roofs of the nave and side aisles. The walls both inside and out are faced with luminous

---

*Moving and recovering stone seem to have been something of a specialty of Buscheto's. The architect went to extraordinary lengths to get his hands on the best of it, and invented machinery to move and rescue it. A thirteenth-century chronicle describes his prowess: "Under the great Buscheto's orders, ten maidens could lift what a thousand oxen could scarcely move, or a freight ship carry on the sea. With his machinery Buscheto could rescue from the bottom of the sea the columns that sank with the ship that carried them on their way from Elba and Sardinia."

white marble and threaded with bands of gray marble, a technique Pisan architects revived from ancient Roman practice as a means to create an illusion of texture on the surface planes. Inside the blind arcades, polychrome lozenge panels of marble are set into the walls. The sculpture of the façade depicts the Evangelists, a host of angels and saints, and beasts both fantastic and real. A Madonna and Child crowns the apex of the roof. Mosaics mark the portals, and bronze doors with fine bas-reliefs fill the threshold. When the light is right and the supporting wall of the façade is cast in shadow, the orders of open arcading, with their array of delicate columns and lush, foliated capitals, appear to float in the landscape in anticipation of an ascent to heaven. The cumulative effect of all this pattern, color, space, light, and shadow is almost Oriental in its abundance and complexity, and it is not far-fetched to suppose that Buscheto may have visited, or at the very least been aware of, some of the exceptional Islamic architecture in the Mediterranean world, including the great mosques of Cordoba and Damascus, the Ibn-Tulun Mosque in Cairo, or the Dome of the Rock in Jerusalem. The note of eastern splendor in Buscheto's scheme is unmistakable, and shows that, commercial and religious rivalry aside, the Muslims were admired and emulated by Europeans for their cultural sophistication, their scientific advances, and the breadth of their learning.

Unlike so many of the Romanesque churches of Germany, Spain, England, and France, which are built of a variety of common, indigenous stone, the use of marble in the construction of the Pisa cathedral and other Tuscan churches of the period—such as San Miniato al Monte in Florence, or San Frediano in Lucca—allowed for a quality that had been virtually absent in the West since the decline of Rome, that of precision. The rough-hewn stone or brick ordinarily employed in early Christian, Byzantine, and Romanesque architecture made for a degree of carelessness of execution and spontaneity that gives these styles an endearing, earthbound character. Not so at Pisa. Here, the white marble Buscheto ordered from Monti Pisani was meant to be as pristine and flawless as Santa Maria Assunta, to whom the duomo is dedicated. Other stone was chosen with equal care: tufa from Livorno was transported by ship along the coast and then up the Arno; limestone from the Verruca was floated down the river. Quarries in Elba which had been abandoned and silent for centuries were reopened to provide Buscheto with the finest stone available.

Along with rough masonry, gone were the simple paleo- or early Christian exteriors virtually bare of embellishment and bound by expediency rather than an artistic vision. The sculpture of the Pisan duomo's western façade is not the work of peasant stone cutters, but of accomplished craftsmen who had traveled and assimilated foreign influences and innovative techniques. The same can be said of the mosaics, the bas-reliefs, and the friezes: they are exotic, kinetic, and vibrant. For all of Buscheto's classical boldness and purity of line, his genius lay in imbuing his cathedral with myriad details—from building materials and architectural elements to decoration—in service of the aesthetic whole. This animated, lively amalgam is what prevents the architect's deceptively simple combination of columns and arcades from growing static and monotonous. "I call *that* Living Architecture," wrote John Ruskin of Buscheto's work. "There is a sensation in every inch of it, and an accommodation to every architectural necessity with a determined variation in arrangement which is exactly like the related proportions and provisions in the structure of organic form." To Ruskin the naturalist, the duomo part was a consummate work of art because he saw it as a living piece of architecture, a vibrant artifact nearly a thousand years old, that somehow never appears dated or archaic. And that is how Buscheto bettered Ulysses and Daedalus: he created a timeless temple that has lost none of its awe-inspiring power.

As Buscheto's vision slowly came to life, so too did Pisa's fortunes. With the definitive defeat of the Muslim forces in Sicily after an exhausting, thirty-year struggle with the Normans, the Mediterranean was no longer divided. Once again, as in the times of Roman hegemony, the local trade routes, and, more important, the principal east–west route that stretched from the Levant to Iberia, were open and relatively safe. The Byzantine fleet protected the eastern Mediterranean and the Aegean, while the Normans, Pisans, and Genoese kept the sea lanes open in the West. The effect of such hard-won and long-awaited security didn't take long to manifest itself, as there soon followed a boom in trade, a frenzy of shipbuilding, a blossoming of an increasingly influential mercantile class, and Europe's first tentative steps toward republicanism, something that had not been seen in the West for centuries. As for Pisa, although it was still nominally under the rule of the marquises of Tuscany, the city came to be regarded and negotiated with as if it were an independent state. Furthermore, in addition to its own code of laws, known as the *Consuetudini di mare,* Pisa also maintained its own magistrate and an executive commission of consuls, the latter deliberately appropriating the title of ancient Rome's most exalted officials in the hopes of bestowing dignity and legitimacy on their fledgling democratic exercise.

Pisa officially escaped Tuscany's domain in 1081, when Holy Roman Emperor Henry IV, on his way back from a long, costly, and unsuccessful siege of Rome (paradoxically, Rome was not a part of the Holy Roman Empire), stopped in at Pisa and granted the city full independence as a commune, in exchange, no doubt, for a tithe for the imperial coffers. Henry's recognition was a blow to feudalism and a triumph for municipal liberty; it also opened a floodgate that no temporal or ecclesiastical power could easily close: by the middle of the twelfth century, there were some three hundred such communes in Italy, all heady with a novel sense of freedom and pinching varying degrees of power and wealth from a legion of bishops, dukes, marquises, popes, and even the emperor himself once he turned his back and returned to Germany. "They possess neither king nor prince to govern them, but only the judges appointed by themselves," wrote a twelfth-century Jewish chronicler of these communes. After centuries of barbarian invasions, feudal oppression, and unremitting battles with the Arabs, Pisa had more than earned its precious autonomy—however fleeting it would prove to be.

When Pope Urban II preached the First Crusade at Clermont in 1095, urging Christians to observe a truce of God at home and march to Jerusalem to wrest the Sepulchre of Christ from the "infidels," the assembled throng met the pontiff's plea with zealous cries of *Deus vult!* ("God wills it!") In Pisa, the reaction to news of the Crusade mixed religious fervor with a considerable dose of glee. For while the First Crusade may well have been a largely French affair—it was, after all, preached on French soil, by a French-born pope, and taken up by mostly French and Norman knights and pilgrims—the Pisans were quick to realize the vast economic potential of an armed, Church-sanctioned expedition to the Holy Land. To begin with, thanks to her endeavors of the past century, Pisa knew a thing or two about the Muslims. In addition, the city had the galleys to ferry Crusader forces and provisions along the complex route to Jerusalem. And finally, the Pisans had an ambitious cleric, Daiberto Lanfranchi, archbishop of Pisa and primate of Corsica—also known in English as Dagobert—to lead the way. By all measures,

Pisa was ideally poised for the Crusades and stood to gain considerable earthly wealth, power, and prestige from them; that Urban was also offering full and complete penance to all Crusaders was an added incentive. The Pisans readied their galleys and prepared to take up the Cross.

While the principal Crusader divisions, under Godfrey of Bouillon, Raymond of Toulouse, and Bohemund of Otranto, elected to trudge across Europe and thus do battle through Asia Minor before they reached Jerusalem (to say nothing of the unsanctioned Crusades undertaken by the ragtag armies of paupers led by Peter the Hermit and Walter the Penniless, which were cut down and literally annihilated by the Turks as soon as they crossed the Bosporus), a Pisan fleet of 120 galleys under the command of Dagobert sailed across the Mediterranean uncontested and arrived on the shores of Palestine in the summer of 1099. There, the Pisan forces were among the first to enter Jerusalem, and one of their number, a Cuccodei Ricucchi, was purportedly the very first to scale the walls.

The Crusaders' taking of Jerusalem can hardly be called a battle; there was little that was glorious about the battle and still less that was praiseworthy about the "chivalrous" knights of the Christian camp. In a frenzy of bloodlust, the Crusaders mercilessly slaughtered Jerusalem's Muslims and Jews, and even some Christians, including women and children; mosques, synagogues, houses, and shops were razed with abandon. The massacre

The Battle of Barbagianni, by Giorgio Vasari (and workshop); from the ceiling of the Salone dei Cinquecento, 1565

was all the more atrocious for the misbegotten religious aura in which it was cloaked. After the carnage, according to William of Tyre, the soldiers "exchanged fresh clothes for those which were blood-stained, and walked barefoot with sighs and tears through the holy places of the city where the Saviour Jesus Christ had trodden as a man, and sweetly kissed the ground which his feet had touched." (Later historians have judged the Crusaders less kindly. In the eighteenth century, for instance, Edward Gibbon tersely wrote: "The knights neglected to live, but were prepared to die, in the service of Christ.")

The Crusaders eventually took control of a total of four cities, establishing the Kingdom of Jerusalem, the County of Edessa, the Principality of Antioch, and the County of Tripoli. Godfrey of Bouillon was elected king of Jerusalem, but would not accept a crown of gold where the Savior had endured a crown of thorns. Nor would he take the title of king, instead preferring the less presumptuous title of "Advocate of the Holy Sepulchre." The Pisan Archbishop Dagobert, meanwhile, was made patriarch, and tried, unsuccessfully, to convert Jerusalem into a theocracy, with himself at the helm of an earthly domain akin to that of the pope in central Italy. Instead, Jerusalem became a vaguely feudal, thoroughly Latin kingdom transposed from the West to the East and imposed by sword and Cross on the Mediterranean shore of Asia. The other Crusader conquests emerged similarly. Naturally, the lifelines between Europe and these Crusader states had to be kept open at all costs. However, because these hastily established crusader fiefs had no proper fleets of their own, they came to rely on Genoa, Pisa, and Venice for their sailing and trading. The maritime republics, of course, were only too happy to oblige, at a premium that typically included a percentage of any booty, control of a quarter in a town where they could settle and set up shop, and freedom from tariffs, tolls, and duties. As it happened, the provisions and conditions extracted by the Italians were often so abusive that they drained the resources of the very state that the Italians had helped to found.

By the early twelfth century, Pisa had used the wealth and influence it had gained to establish consuls in Acre, Alexandria, Damietta, Armenia, Salerno, and Naples, as well as colonies in Antioch, Tripoli, Tyre, and Jaffa, and even in the North African cities of Bona, Bugia, and Tunis. In 1111, not even fifty years after it had emerged from obscurity to take Palermo from the Muslims and a dozen years since its arrival in the far eastern Mediterranean, Pisa concluded a commercial treaty with Byzantine emperor Alexius I that granted free transit of Pisan trade to the Holy Land and the concession of a port of call and a Pisan quarter in Constantinople, an ideal interim port between Pisa and the Holy Land. Venice and Genoa likewise had concessions and colonies and quarters of their own. Suddenly, the Mediterranean seemed like an Italian sea. "These three cities had more vessels on the Mediterranean than the whole of Christendom besides," wrote the nineteenth-century Swiss historian Jean Sismondi, in *Histoire des Républiques Italiennes du moyen âge*.

Alas, it did not take long for these new, aggressive republics to come to blows among themselves or with anyone else whom they perceived to be impinging on their trade. Pisa and Genoa were at constant odds over Sardinia and Corsica and would fight intermittently for centuries; Venice loathed Pisa, and Genoa was suspicious of rival Venice. As if that were not enough, newcomers who tried to carve out a share of the Mediterranean trade did so at their own risk, as Amalfi discovered to its detriment. In 1136, Pisa raided Amalfi by surprise, looted and torched the town, and made off with, among other spoils, the Pandects, a digest of civil law compiled for the great Byzantine emperor Justinian. Amalfi's galleys, it seemed, had been growing too familiar a sight around the Tyrrhenian Sea.

Meanwhile, the First Crusade and those that followed (the "Crusader spirit," after all, infected Europe for roughly three hundred years) created a fascination in the West for all things Eastern, and in the markets of Italy, Germany, France, and England, there was an unrelenting demand for the refined splendors of the Orient. Pisan galleys returned to port with goods the likes of which Europeans had not seen since the glory days of Rome, if ever—fine furniture, silks, glass, metalwork, ivory, spices, and precious stones. The trade made the city fantastically rich: merchants became princes, the fleet of galleys grew, palaces went up along the banks of the Arno, and the city acquired a new cosmopolitan air—all this when Florence and Siena were still mere market towns. To some, this new, worldly Pisa was abhorrent, a view expressed by the monk Dorizone in Bernardo Maragone's *Annales pisani:* "Those going to Pisa will see sea monsters; the city is sullied by Pagans, Turks, Libyans, and also Parthians and Chaldees that visit its shores." Those with a better eye and more generous spirit described an altogether different scene: "Pisa is a metropolis of the Rum [the Romans]," wrote the Arab geographer al-Idrisi in the twelfth century, "renowned is its name and wide its territory; it has rich markets and well-kept houses, roomy promenades and extensive countryside full of gardens and orchards and uninterrupted crops . . . high are the fortresses, fertile the land, abundant the waters, and wonderful the monuments."

Al-Idrisi would have seen Buscheto's monumental duomo, but, alas, while it was still a work in progress. The architect died before the cathedral was finished, and it remained incomplete even when it was finally consecrated by Pope Gelasius II in 1118. Work proceeded at a steady pace under the architect Rainaldo, but progress was slow on account of the sheer scale of Buscheto's plan. Meanwhile, Pisa's burgeoning wealth and pride inspired a civic compulsion to build more monuments in testament to its grandeur and might. Accordingly, in 1153, ground was broken for the new baptistery in the Campo dei Miracoli, squarely facing Buschato's cathedral façade. Its architect was Deotisalvi, who had already built the church of the Holy Sepulchre in Pisa and Lucca's Church of San Cristoforo. His baptistery for the Campo dei Miracoli is circular in plan, and, in its initial stages at least, replicated the same architectural idiom, the blind arcades and progressive orders of delicate columns, found in Buscheto's cathedral. Sadly, later Gothic additions, including a host of incongruous pinnacles and gables and a hideous, teatlike dome, greatly diminished the baptistery's original beauty, but its presence in the Campo dei Miracoli and its position vis-à-vis the duomo shows that the Pisans had a grand architectural vision for the cathedral square. Not since the magnificent forums of ancient Rome had such a forceful yet finely etched architectural statement emerged in the West.

Then, as construction on the cathedral and the baptistery was under way, a new edifice was planned for the conjunction; it would go up in the shadows of the cathedral's eastern façade but would nevertheless form an integral part of the whole architectural scheme. It was, of course, the campanile. With its bells it would draw the faithful, and from its lofty heights it would provide a privileged view across the monumental Campo dei Miracoli and all that Pisa was building. The campanile would be both a bell tower and a tribune—or at least that was the intention of its anonymous architect.

FOUR

Terreni Limosi

campanil-e *m.* bell tower; *amóre di-,* love of one's native town or village.

-ismo *m.* parochialism.

—*The Cambridge Italian Dictionary* (1962)

L est anyone should ever doubt that it was he who had created "this marble church which has no equal," Buscheto signed the cathedral with his tomb. Deotisalvi left his mark as well, though his testament is decidedly less emphatic than that of the braggart Buscheto: two of the baptistery's pilasters bear the simple engraving DEOTISALVI MAGISTER HUIUS OPERIS, or, "Deotisalvi master of this work." The campanile, by contrast, while the best-known of the edifices which rise up in the Campo dei Miracoli, is, paradoxically, wholly anonymous; there is no signature or inscription, no epitaph or monogram, nor, indeed, any extant document to reveal the identity of the tower's architect. An inscription in the entrance to the campanile simply reads, AN. DNI. MCLXXIIII. CAMPANILE. HOC. FUIT. FUN-

*DATU. MSE. AUG.** The name of the architect of so important a building is conspicuously absent—as if no one wanted to recognize this bastard child among lofty, acknowledged siblings. Not that there haven't been candidates for the paternity of the tower. A longstanding tradition, accepted by the sixteenth-century master architect Giorgio Vasari, for example, points to Bonnano Pisano, the sculptor of the cathedral's original bronze doors (themselves destroyed in a devastating fire in 1595). Others claim that the tower, like the baptistery, was designed by Deotisalvi, owing to the architectural affinity of the two buildings, or by his overshadowed collaborator Gerardo. Still another theory, more fanciful and thoroughly erroneous, attributes the campanile to maestro William of Innsbruck, a hunchback who supposedly built the tower askew out of spite borne of his own flawed condition. All of these hypotheses are purely speculative, and one rather hopes that the mystery is never resolved and the authorship of the tower remains an enigma.

Yet while the architect of the Tower of Pisa may be unknown, its benefactor is not. In 1172, a Pisan widow

---

*"This campanile was founded in the month of August A.D. 1174." Pisans and Florentines dated the beginning of the year *ab incarnatione,* that is, from the 25th of March. The Florentines, however, dated it from the 25th following, and the Pisans from the 25th of March preceding, the start of the common year. The new or common style, also known as the Roman style, was adopted throughout Tuscany in 1750. The Tower of Pisa, therefore, was begun in 1173 of the common calendar.

named Berta di Bernardo left "sixty coins" (of what metal is not clear, but the Italian cities, like the Byzantines, favored gold coinage) in her will and testament for the purchase of stone to build the campanile. Thus, in contrast to the cathedral's foundation laid with the spoils of war, the campanile seems to be the product of a genuine act of benevolence and piety—though the more cynical might call it buying one's way to salvation. A rage for bell towers, as it happens, was one of the most notable architectural manifestations of the Church's medieval *renovatio*. The campaniles, like the bells in the steeples of churches in the north and west of Europe (and the human *muezzin* in the minarets of the Islamic world), were meant to beckon the faithful and keep them vigilant in their religious rites and obligations; bells summoned the flock to Mass, reminded them to recite the prayers of the Angelus, and, in a stroke of finality, sounded the death knell. A medieval distich praised the roll of bells thusly:

> *Funera plango, fulgura frango, Sabbata pango,*
> *Excito lentos, dissipo ventos, paco cruentos.*
> *(I mourn for death, I break the lightning, I fix the*
> *   Sabbath,*
> *I rouse the lazy, I scatter the winds, I appease the cruel.)*

Curiously enough, despite the early-second-millennium vogue, bell towers were hardly new. The campanile of Sant' Apollinare Nuovo in Ravenna, the earliest recorded example of one, dates from the sixth century. The old St. Peter's also had a campanile, stout and square in plan, but it was demolished in the sixteenth century by order of Pope Nicholas V to make way for the new basilica. Still, bell towers never seemed to have inspired undue enthusiasm until the twelfth and thirteenth centuries, when literally hundreds of campaniles sprang up all over Italy like so many proclamations of a rejuvenated faith. Rome alone boasted dozens, many of which, like those of Santa Maria in Cosmedin, Santa Francesca Romana, and Santa Maria in Trastevere, still survive and have become indelible features of the Eternal City's landscape. Of course, Pisa too succumbed to the tower fever, the Campo dei Miracoli would be incomplete without one, but little did the widow Berta di Bernardo know that her legacy of sixty coins would go to building a tower that would become a universal architectural icon and the most distinctive symbol that Pisa would ever know.

When it came time to situate the future campanile in the Campo dei Miracoli, the anonymous architect selected a spot deemed propitious for a number of reasons, none of them coincidental. The tower would rise up between the cathedral's apse and its southeast transept, from which point its replication of the circular volumes of both the nearby apse and the farther-off but still visible baptistery would make for a profound sense of architectural and aesthetic coherence and continuity. Spatially, the campanile would be close enough to the duomo to share the same visual frame, but at the same time, it would stand distant enough to prevent the reverberations of its bells from damaging the cathedral's structural integrity. Furthermore, the tower would stand at the crucial juncture of the Campo dei Miracoli and the via Santa Maria, the principal thoroughfare which leads from the city center to the cathedral square, and hence it would mark the entrance to the square. Just behind the site ran the ancient via Aemilia. From the campanile's heights, observers would be able to capture the panorama of Pisa. They could view everything going on in the piazza below, be it ecclesiastical pomp or more secular pageantry; they could see who and what was coming in and out of the square; and they could look out over the city to take in an expanse of rooftops, lesser towers, the odd cupola, and, in the distance, the masts and sails of galleys plying the Arno.

Had Deotisalvi and the campanile's architect not chosen to follow the schematic and stylistic motifs set down by Buscheto in the cathedral, the Campo dei Miracoli might have been a very different place, and this great conjunction of monuments might not have been a conjunction at all, but rather a study in discord. As it was, the architects working in Pisa seem to have shared a common aesthetic and a desire to project a collective architectural vision distinctly their own. The Pisan Romanesque, like the Romanesque movement throughout western Europe, drew its inspiration from a host of architectural sources—Rome, Byzantium, Lombardy, and Islam among them—but nowhere did the synthesis evolve as power- fully and with such spatial eloquence as at Pisa. What's more, the great majority of architects, artists, and crafts- men working in and around the Campo dei Miracoli were native Pisans: the city did not rely on outside talent to embellish its landscape, but developed an organic school of its own. Not only in trade routes, ever- burgeoning markets, and fabulous mercantile riches did Pisa's greatness lie; the true measure of Pisa's greatness may be found in its artists' creation of some of the most inspired and flawless works of architecture and art of the Middle Ages. Pisans had the Carthaginian spirit, to be sure, but they were similarly blessed with a rare aesthetic genius. While most architects elsewhere in western Europe were still working in rough-hewn stone and struggling with the structural problems of the groined vault, Pisan builders were building with the confidence and aplomb of the ancients.

Fittingly, the design of the campanile was at once auda- cious and in perfect harmony with the duomo; it called for a solid base of blind arcades topped by six orders of grace- ful open arcades, all crowned by a belfry at the eighth order. The composition of open arcading, which forms a fragile veil of marble around the interior supporting wall, is nothing less than a rendering of Buscheto's cathedral façade in cylindrical form. Most of the other Italian cam- paniles of the period, as well as those of earlier eras, rose in blind stories of unplastered brown brick with wall faces divided vertically by pilaster strips and blind arcades, as in the campanile of San Marco in Venice, or horizontally by cornices and corbel tables, as in the tower at Milan's San Satiro. Only at the upper, or belfry, story did these campaniles open to a gallery or arcade embellished with columns and capitals; what preceded the belfry was deemed of little importance and its role was almost purely structural. One climbed these towers in almost utter darkness, with no stopping-off places, no access to the exterior until one reached the belfry. The design of the Pisan campanile, however, was revolutionary, and whoever the architect was, he approached the project with a certain measure of defiance. Although his tower would have to support the weight of seven colossal bronze bells, the structure itself would appear weightless, an effect achieved via architectural sleight of hand. With the exception of the ground story and the belfry, the Pisan campanile's six intervening orders would consist of open galleries, each defined by a ring of thirty columns bearing mostly foliated and protomai* capitals and uniform rounded arches. The tower would be exposed, almost transparent, and its spaces would be delineated not by solid, concealing walls, but by a crop of columns. The structure would be, as it were, a column of columns. If the blind brick façades of campaniles such as that of San Marco were intended to impart stability

*A protomai capital is one with half-figures, sometimes human, often animal, projecting from its four corners.

and, by association, the sense of a stalwart faith, the design of the Tower of Pisa sought to convey something quite different, namely, lightness and a kind of magical, otherworldly spirit. And if only to confirm just how deceptive appearances can sometimes be, it is worth noting that at 9:47 A.M. on July 14, 1902, the campanile of San Marco collapsed without warning; the cause of the downfall was said to be a combination of age and excess weight—in a phrase, death by natural causes.

With the commencement of work on the Pisan campanile, the construction of the baptistery in full swing, and Buscheto's duomo progressing ever so slowly to a finish, the Campo dei Miracoli became an enormous building site teeming with craftsmen, artisans, and laborers, all working dutifully to realize Pisa's monuments to its own splendor. The architectural enterprise was the responsibility of the Opera della Primaziale, also known as the Opera del Duomo or the Opera di Santa Maria, an organization established expressly to administer and manage the complex works in the Campo dei Miracoli. At the helm of the Opera was the *operarius* or *operaio,* who saw to the considerable building funds, canvassed relentlessly for donations, and wrangled with the bishop on the one hand, and the *capomagister,* or head architect, on the other. For his part, the capomagister was responsible for the work in progress and the fate and efficiency of the workers, among whom were carpenters and metalworkers, smiths and barrowmen, gilders and painters, various foremen, assorted clerks, and a man of the cloth to see to the workers' spiritual needs. Yet the true masters of this medieval workforce, and the ones who most concerned the capomagister, were undoubtedly the masons, stone-cutters, and sculptors. The sound of the mason's hammer striking stone, in fact, was something of a clarion call for the masses of humanity caught up in the cathedral boom of the Middle Ages. It was the mason who sought out the quarry, selected and cut the huge blocks of stone from the landscape, fashioned the stone into smaller blocks and columns and cornices and various other architectural elements, sculpted delicate figures and motifs from the hardest marbles, and finally put all of this stone into place. No architectural scheme could even be imagined and certainly no consummate work of art realized without the most skilled masons and sculptors. As it happened, Pisa produced just such men in abundance. The Campo dei Miracoli was the best school an apprentice mason could dream of and a mark of excellence on the work record of any stonecutter or sculptor. To have worked at Pisa, and news of the project had spread far and wide, imparted a certain cachet. It should be no surprise, then, to know that Pisan masons and sculptors who worked in the Campo dei Miracoli later went on to work at churches throughout Tuscany and in Sicily, Sardinia, and Corsica. In Florence, for example, the baptistery (called "il bel San Giovanni" by Dante) was built entirely by Pisan masons.

The lion's share of the marble used to adorn the Campo dei Miracoli was cut from the quarries around San Giuliano, northeast of Pisa. San Giuliano marble is a lustrous and resilient stone, and among Pisan masons it was the stone of choice. Transporting ponderous loads of stone, of course, was a Herculean task, and as slow as it was dangerous, but in 1160, the Pisans, ever attuned to the watery element, built a canal through the marshes northeast of the city to link Pisa directly to the quarries. Henceforth, some of the best marble in Italy floated to Pisa. This seemingly innocuous advance in transportation can be more readily appreciated when one considers the sheer quantity of stone employed in the Campo dei Miracoli: for the campanile alone, an edifice far smaller than the baptistery and dwarfed by the duomo, the masons needed enough stone to shape 32,240 blocks with which to face the interior and exterior walls of the structural cylinder, 15 half columns for the ground story, 180 columns for the arcades, 12 columns for the belfry, column bases and capitals, hundreds of arches, vaults, corbels, and jambs, and, finally, 293 steps for the interior stairwell. All of it, mind you, had to be cut, extracted, divided, shaped, hoisted, and set by hand. That the stone could at least be shipped to Pisa relatively effortlessly was a blessing.

More than a year and a half before the August 9, 1173, official groundbreaking for the campanile, the architect, or master builder, of the tower was already in San Giuliano with his *taglia** in tow, meticulously choosing the stone for this third monument to rise up in the Campo dei Miracoli. Presumably, the widow Berta di Bernardo's sixty coins could buy a good bit of stone. The purest, least-flawed marble was reserved for the columns, capitals, and exterior ashlar blocks; pieces of *bardiglio,* a marble streaked with gray, were set aside for the signature horizontal bands favored by the Pisan architects of the period. Some of this marble was worked *in situ* at the quarry, but the best blocks were transported to Pisa and left in a warehouse built in the cathedral square, where the marble was allowed to mature, or *purificantur,* as the Pisans said. As might be expected after millions of years embedded in the earth, a marble's reaction to light and air, cold and heat, rain, frost, and snow, could be unpredictable at best. No master mason worth his chisel would work freshly quarried stone, particularly for such an important commission. Thus, they waited and watched the marble mature and began to imagine which blocks would furnish columns, which would make a rounded arch. The scrupulous care that the Pisan masons devoted to their marble was telling of a craft just beginning to take on the more rigorous air of a fine art. The master masons—or *lapicidi,* carvers of decorations and sculptures in stone, as they were sometimes

---

*A *taglia* was a school or circle of masons, stonecutters, and sculptors, along with other craftsmen and apprentices, which developed around a master builder or architect.

called—weren't merely shaping rude blocks of stone but chiseling exquisite capitals, increasingly refined figures, and the slenderest of columns from unsullied marble. Theirs was a profession of prestige and modest prosperity, and one which allowed for a considerable measure of freedom, at least by strict medieval standards. Not surprisingly, the descendants of some of these accomplished artisans went on to form a circle of Pisan sculptors in the thirteenth and fourteenth centuries, the great Giovanni Pisano among them, who in turn, were the artistic precursors of Renaissance artists such as Lorenzo Ghiberti, Donatello, and Bernardo Rossellino. Emerging in the Campo dei Miracoli were not only three splendid monuments, but a whole cultural landscape sown with the seeds of prospective genius.

Before the craftsmen and laborers could begin work on the campanile, they were obliged to take this oath of fealty and good faith to the Opera della Primaziale: "I, Benato Bottici," recited one such craftsman, "pledge to be solicitous and attentive in the building of the campanile of the cathedral, in accordance with the means of the Opera." The oath was intended to keep a varied workforce in line and accountable for their labors, for in among the ablest artisans there were a good many journeyman laborers too, unskilled, poorly paid, and often less than diligent. If things went wrong on the building site, as they invariably did, what with accidental deaths and serious injuries, not to mention fights, delays, and protests, the blame was usually laid squarely on these itinerant laborers. For centuries, in fact, it was widely believed that the Tower of Pisa stood askew as a result of shabby medieval workmanship, or that the laborers deliberately undermined the construction to protest their meager wages. Rubbish: the workmanship displayed in the campanile is irreproachable and astonishingly refined for the age. There is nothing to admonish about the realization of the tower, and no justification whatever in pointing an accusatory finger at the common workers.

Now, whether or not the tower's architect was required to take such an oath is impossible to say, but it is clear that he too was solicitous and attentive—at least most of the time. On paper, the campanile is a miracle of minute calculations and seamless proportions. Its design is modular, that is, it is based on a uniform component, in this case the columns of the galleries, and all other elements in the construction are proportionate to it. The columns measure ten Pisan feet (a Pisan foot is roughly equivalent to the Roman foot that provided a widespread standard of measurement before the metric system was adopted in the nineteenth century), while the circumference of the tower is one hundred Pisan feet and its height one hundred *braccia,* or arms, precisely. There is nothing haphazard about these figures; they were calculated with the assiduousness of the architects of the classical world. The tower's fatal flaw lay deeper.

That the campanile was to be built on unstable ground

was no surprise to the architect or any other builder in Pisa; shifty alluvial terrain, *terreni limosi,* was, and still is, a common occurrence in the region and foundations were calculated accordingly. There were plenty of other buildings off kilter in Pisa, even other towers and campaniles, but neither the cathedral nor the baptistery had suffered any variation due to the precariousness of the ground in the Campo dei Miracoli, in part because of the inordinate care taken in laying the foundations of these monuments. At least part of the reason for the baptistery and the campanile being round in plan, in fact, was precisely to offset the precariousness of the ground in the Campo dei Miracoli. Round structures distribute weight and stress in a more even manner, while rectangular or square structures suffer undue thrust at the corners, where they tend eventually to break up first.

When work began on the campanile on August 9, it was specifically to dig the vast excavation for the tower's foundation. Following the orders of Bonnano Pisano, Deotisalvi, Gerardo, or whoever the architect of the campanile was, laborers dug to a depth of approximately three meters and poured a foundation of concrete composed mostly of quartzite stone. The foundation was then left to settle and solidify for a good many months, as was the custom in Pisa. Meanwhile, masons and sculptors went on carving the architectural elements—columns, corbels, capitals, and the like—which would soon be put together like so many pieces of a puzzle.

At last, the building of the campanile proper com-
menced in early 1174, two years from the death of the
widow Berta di Bernardo. The ground story rose in blind
arcades and half columns around a base wall which, like
those of the duomo and the baptistery, measured no less
than thirteen feet thick. The structural integrity of the
tower's base order was crucial, as it would have to withstand not only the weight of seven upper stories and seven
bronze bells, but the potentially stone-shattering vibrations
produced by the latter. Meanwhile, growing up the interior
of the tower were the first steps of a grand spiral staircase
that would be wide enough, it was said, to climb the campanile on horseback.

Workers also added adornments as they built. Besides
the decorative motifs appropriated from the cathedral,
which included the alternating bands of white and gray
marble and the polychrome lozenges set inside the blind
arcades, the masons inscribed the tower with a number of
curious symbols, figures, and inscriptions. Flanking the
entrance door, a place of obvious importance, they carved
two zoomorphic reliefs depicting wild beasts giving chase
to a fantastic winged serpent. Nearby, another relief
showed two galleys entering the Pisan port beneath an
immense tower, a symbol of Pisa's nautical and architectural mastery. Grotesque monkeys chained back to back
were deemed a fitting subject for a singular capital. They
also included the foundational inscription—informative, if
unenlightening, but again, no signature of any architect.

When workers reached the height of the first cornice, they realized that the foundation had shifted ever so slightly to the north. It signaled nothing alarming, mind you, but enough of a variation to prompt the architect to create a weightier cornice for the south side of the tower in an attempt to coax the base order back to level. Such remedial measures were common enough in the fickle Pisan terrain, and no one seemed unduly concerned. Thereafter, work proceeded at a rate of approximately a year and a half per story, or order of galleries. By 1178, then, the tower was approximately halfway built, with three orders of open galleries atop the solid ground story. From what could be seen, this campanile, as all those who came to gaze in awe at the architectural feats of the Campo dei Miracoli could tell, would be a fine complement to the duomo and the baptistery. If one's campanile was a measure of local pride or *campanilismo,* they reasoned, then Pisa would be forever admired and envied in equal parts. . . .

And then the whole towering exploit came to a sudden, bewildering halt. Works on the campanile were suspended; the masons were dismissed; journeymen moved on to building sites in Lucca, Siena, or perhaps Pistoia. Pisa was left with a truncated tower and a correspondingly diminished sense of *campanilismo.*

No one knows with certainty quite why the tower would stand idle for nearly a century. Documentary evidence for the period is both slight and ambiguous. In the archives of the Opera della Primaziale, there is an extract from the Pisan statutes, penned on parchment and dating from the decade between 1190 and 1200, which reads, *"Costitutum pro opera et Pisane Civitatis"* ("Built by the efforts of the Pisan citizens"), followed by the date of the campanile's foundation. Nothing illuminating in those words, though in the left margin, the scribe also saw fit to render the tower as it then stood. While he was no architectural draftsman, his sure hand drew a tower four stories tall with a slight, but unmistakable, inclination. Nonetheless, no actual mention is made of the works being suspended, never mind on what possible account. Some have claimed that a hiatus in construction was a common practice, imposed to allow buildings to settle farther in unstable ground. Others suspect that the campanile's masons may have simply exhausted their supply of stone; evidence for this may be the fact that there is a noticeable decline in the quality of the stone above the fourth order. In the absence of more definitive clues, the most plausible explanation for the prolonged halt in construction would still seem to be a sudden and dramatic shift in the terrain—unless, of course, one were to look beyond the tower and its immediate environs and focus instead on the shrinking fortunes of Pisa during the long years in which the campanile stood stunted and silent.

Since the beginning of the eleventh century, Pisa had been blessed with a string of military victories, increasingly prosperous trade, an advantageous role in the Crusades, and the blossoming liberties of a commune. The Empire of

Sails, as the city became known, was enjoying a golden age, even as the signs of an eventual and inevitable decline already loomed on the empire's rather overextended horizons. A host of rivals and successors was either waiting in the wings or doing its best to hasten the fall; as may well be expected, Pisa had not reaped commercial, military, and political success without creating some very powerful enemies. Lucca, an ancient overlord and Pisa's closest neighbor, was the city's most inveterate enemy; a war between the two cities in 1003, in fact, was the first waged between medieval Italian cities. Moreover, Pisa was at constant odds with Genoa over Sardinia, Corsica, and ports and sea lanes all over the Mediterranean. These rivals had joined forces on numerous occasions against the Arabs and on Crusade in the Holy Land, it's true, but as soon as their common enemies were eliminated, they were quick to renew old hatreds. Venice too was a fierce competitor for Levantine trade, and it was jealous of Pisa's privileges in the ports of Byzantium. And landlocked Florence, every year growing more powerful as a commercial, industrial, and financial center, felt understandably constricted by Pisa's control of the Arno and so the former's outlet to the sea. These were too many cunning enemies on too many distant fronts, and by the thirteenth century, Pisa began to find itself increasingly alone and on the defensive. It was during this time that an adage was coined and came to spread among Pisa's foes: "Better a corpse in the house than a Pisan at the door." Nor was the enmity confined merely to homespun proverbs. Dante Alighieri, a poet and Florentine patriot, spared no invective when it came to Pisa. As he wrote:

Ah, Pisa! foulest blemish on the land
where "si" sounds sweet and clear, since those nearby
    you
are slow to blast the ground on which you stand,
may Caprara and Gorgona drift from place
and dam the flooding Arno at its mouth
until it drowns the last of your foul race!

The Inferno, Canto XXXIII

Considering what Pisa endured in the thirteenth century, it is little wonder that works on the campanile came to a halt and weren't renewed for close to a hundred years. The century began with a resounding defeat of the Pisan fleet at the hands of the Venetians as the latter besieged Byzantium, curiously enough, en route to the Fourth Crusade; as a result, Pisa was forced to surrender its commercial privileges in Constantinople and many of its safe harbors throughout the Aegean. Then, in 1220, the newly crowned Holy Roman Emperor, Frederick II, obliged Pisa to relinquish half of Corsica to Genoa. Two years later, fiercely Ghibelline Pisa was routed on the battlefield at Castel del Bosco by a Guelph alliance led by Florence and Lucca. This unaccustomed defeat was only the first of many clashes in the prolonged, internecine Ghibelline-Guelph struggle—the clash of opposing political parties that pitted emperor against pope, nobles against burghers, and brother against brother, and would eventually seal Pisa's demise. Nor did it help that to its legion of enemies Pisa unwisely added the pope: when the Pisan fleet captured and held for ransom a convoy of French prelates escorted by the Genoese on their way to Rome in 1241 to dethrone Frederick II, Pope Gregory IX hurled an interdict, or decree that excludes a person or community from participating in most of the holy sacraments and from receiving Christian burial, on the whole of Pisa. More misfortune followed, more defeats at the hands of Florence and Lucca, more territory and concessions lost. Pisa rebounded briefly in 1260 with an epic victory at Montaperti, in which fifteen thousand Ghibellines, mostly Pisans and Sienese, backed by Florentine political exiles and a handful of King Manfred's German knights, destroyed an imposing Guelph army forty thousand strong. The triumph, however, was short-lived; six years later, Pisa was again vanquished, this time at Benevento. And then Rudolf of Hapsburg assumed the Holy Roman imperial throne in 1273, and promptly acknowledged full papal power in Sardinia, thus wresting from Pisa one of the jewels in its Tyrrhenian crown. In the light of such relentless calamities, it would seem logical that no one was thinking much of the intricacies of the campanile. The monuments in the Campo dei Miracoli were conceived for the greater glory of Pisa, and now the Empire of Sails appeared to be sinking irremediably in a storm-tossed sea.

FIVE

Unfinished Business

"To see Pisa, you must now go to Genoa."

— A popular saying which arose in the wake of the 1284 Battle of Meloria, in which Pisa lost most of its fleet and saw 11,000 of its men led off in chains to the dungeons of Genoa

A century is tantamount to an eternity for any edifice to languish incomplete and misshapen. In one hundred years, aesthetic tastes change, enthusiasms wax and wane, building techniques develop and advance, and architects seek new paradigms and motifs, or resurrect old ones, to give their age its proper expression in stone. When the Tower of Pisa was at last resuscitated in 1272, after ninety-eight years in a near-fatal stupor, the Campo dei Miracoli was no longer quite the same. The baptistery now bore crocketed gables and pinnacles, the cathedral dome had sprouted finials, and there was talk of building a monumental cemetery with a cloister of tracery-filled arches. A new style, the Gothic, had arrived from the north, via France and Germany, and taken a restrained but clear hold in the hitherto pure Romanesque geography of the cathedral square. The Gothic revolution would eventually leave its mark on all of the monuments in the Campo dei Miracoli—except, thankfully, the campanile.

The Tower of Pisa's new master was Giovanni di Simone, *capomagister,* or master builder, of the Opera del Duomo and an undisputed favorite of the Pisan archbishop Federico Visconti. The archbishop had turned to him when Pope Alexander IV agreed to lift the Pisan interdict of 1241 on condition that the city build a hospital; soon after, the architect was planning the Camposanto Monumentale, the magnificent cemetery complex that would complete the Campo dei Miracoli. He was determined to tackle the tower too.

Giovanni di Simone found the campanile half finished and already tilting noticeably to the south, but to just what degree it is hard to say. The lean was pronounced enough, however, for the architect to project the remaining fifth-, sixth-, and seventh-story galleries at a corrective, northerly tilt in order to bring the tower back to the perpendicular and its true axis. Such a plan would mean that the campanile would no longer be rectilinear, but concave, resulting in a bananalike shape. Aesthetically, Giovanni di Simone remained resolutely faithful to the campanile's original scheme, and declined to carry out the upper orders in any sort of new, Gothic plan. Perhaps the tower's design was too precise and decisive to allow for any frivolous additions or alterations, no matter how

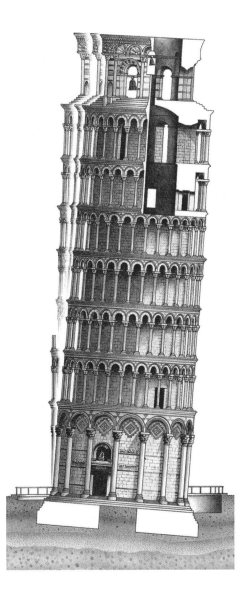

pervasive the architectural fashion or what was evolving elsewhere in the Campo dei Miracoli. Whatever the motive, di Simone's work betrays no concessions to Gothicism. Under his watch, the campanile materialized, all minor remedial devices aside, in an unadulteratedly Pisan Romanesque style, just as it had been conceived. By abiding slavishly to the tower's original plan, however, Giovanni di Simone also missed a singular opportunity, if not exactly to set the campanile straight, at least to relieve its suffering. The architect neglected to build the walls of the upper three orders of galleries any less substantially than those below and in so doing diminish the excessive weight and pressure on the foundation and subsoil below it. The campanile's original sin, in other words, continued to go unchecked, and as the years passed and building proceeded, the structure grew only weightier and weightier. The *terreni limosi* reacted accordingly, and the tower continued to bow perceptibly to the south.

By 1278, the works had reached the height of the seventh cornice, and the eight-story belfry was all that remained to be built. Bells were being cast in the foundries of Campania.* But as fate would have it, just when it appeared that Pisa would at last get its cherished

---

*Both *campanile* and *campana,* the Italian word for *bell,* have their etymological root in Campania, the Italian province once home to the best bronze foundries.

campanile, the works once again came to a sudden, inexplicable halt. Soon after, a single bell was provisionally installed inside the tower at the seventh story, but without the open plan of a belfry, the bell rang muffled and uncertain.

With the tower stalled indefinitely, Giovanni di Simone turned his full attention to the Camposanto Monumentale, the sprawling cloister and cemetery complex that he was building on the cathedral's northern flank. Since the duomo was founded in 1063, the tombs and graves of Pisa's noble and ecclesiastic luminaries had been accumulating around the periphery of the cathedral, and the terrain had grown crowded and, well, grim. The Camposanto would gather all of these old, eminent bones under one roof, as it were. For Giovanni di Simone, the Camposanto must have presented a far more engaging commission than the completion of the campanile, and one can not help but think that the architect was relieved, if not delighted, to have the headaches of the tower behind him. To begin with, the cemetery was his own work and not that of a long-gone, and even by then perhaps forgotten, architect of another age, as was the tower, where his role was confined largely to corrective measures. Nor did the Camposanto require dealing with any of the technical obstacles inherent in the shifting Pisan terrain. The cemetery structure is an elongated, single-story cloister, rectangular in plan, and its weight is distributed horizontally. If any portion of the cloister's foundation were to give way, the breach would have to be corrected, naturally, but it would hardly jeopardize the stability of the whole structure. Compared to the campanile, the Camposanto was relatively painless, at least from a structural point of view.

Di Simone's attention to his own project, even if at the expense of the campanile, was not in vain. The affinity of the Camposanto with the other monuments in the Campo dei Miracoli is manifest in its decorative motifs and the geometric clarity of its white marble. The expansive façade of the cloister, composed of blind arcades and interrupted only by two openings for thresholds, appears almost contemporary to the twenty-first-century observer in its spareness and provides a stunning backdrop to the duomo and baptistery. And like the other edifices in the square, the Camposanto was conceived on a scale of almost imperial proportions. Despite being faced with war, mounting enemies, and shrinking markets, thirteenth-century Pisa still not only built as if the republic would last a thousand years, but with a grandiosity that sometimes approached the absurd. Fifty-three shiploads of earth were brought from Mount Calvary in Jerusalem to fill the interior courtyard of the Camposanto, for example, to assure that departed Pisans would forever rest in thoroughly hallowed ground. There was something decadent about the gesture, to be sure, but also something strangely prescient—as if by preparing a cemetery of such extravagance, the Pisans could already sense their impending demise amid all the splendor that was growing up around them.

Alas, Giovanni di Simone would die before the Camposanto (not to mention the campanile) was completed. The sculptor Giovanni Pisano succeeded him as capomagister, and Pisano and his *taglia* gave the cloister its delicate tracery and the magnificent Gothic tabernacle crowning its entrance. Later, Taddeo Gaddi and Andrea Orcagna—both, curiously enough, Florentines—would paint the interior walls with sumptuous, if chilling, frescoes depicting, fittingly, the biblical stories of Job and the Crucifixion, as well as the Triumph of Death, the Last Judgment, and, finally, Hell.

August 6, the feast of San Sisto, is not a date which Pisans tend to forget. The day is commemorated for both a brilliant victory, namely the assault on Palermo in 1063, which provided the spoils for the founding of the duomo, as well as an appalling defeat, that of the battle of Meloria in 1284, which spelled Pisa's ruin as a naval power. Accordingly, San Sisto is a feast tinged with equal measures of pride and remorse. In the 221 years separating the brilliant victory and the ignoble defeat of San Sisto's day, Pisa had enjoyed a prominent place on the medieval stage. And given that it had found its glory and riches at sea during that era, it seems only appropriate that there too, on the sea, the republic would meet its end.

On Sunday, August 6, 1284, the whole of the Genoese fleet, comprising eighty-eight galleys, appeared before Meloria, a rocky islet off the Pisan coast. For centuries, the two rival maritime republics had been competing for sovereignty over Corsica and Sardinia and dominance in the Tyrrhenian Sea, and had come to blows time and again, but never definitively. This engagement at Meloria looked to be another scene in their long-running, violent drama, played out not on a dusty battlefield, but at sea, where the two were in their element and where their true power lay. Accordingly, the Genoese arrived with a plan. In order to draw the Pisans out of their well-protected harbor, Uberto Doria, the Genoese admiral, divided his forces into two parallel lines facing the coast. The first, which he himself commanded, consisted of the bulk of his fleet, while the second line was stationed far enough behind the first so that the Pisans were unable to determine whether it was made up of more galleys of war or simply smaller support craft, yet close enough to the first line to strike quickly and turn the tide in battle.

Before sailing out to meet its foe, the Pisan fleet of seventy-two galleys was blessed by the archbishop. As it happened, the silver cross of the prelate's staff fell into the Arno during the benediction, but rather than heed the omen—superstition was rife even then among sailors—the Pisans declared that if the wind was in their favor, they could do without divine intervention. Thus, with the city's podestà,* Alberto Morosini, at the helm of their flagship, the Pisan galleys sailed out in a frontal attack against what they believed to be the first and only line of Genoese ships, and proceeded to do battle in the usual medieval fashion, that is, by ram and board. Initially, the battle was close enough, but soon Admiral Doria's strategy unfolded and the second Genoese line set upon the Pisan flank. From that point, it was a rout: contemporary chroniclers write of five thousand Pisan dead and eleven thousand prisoners, including the podestà. Only a handful of vessels managed to retreat and limp back to port under the command of Ugolino della Gherardesca,† one of Morosini's lieutenants, but the rest of the Pisan fleet was annihilated.

---

*"Podestà" (from Latin *potestas,* "power") was the title of a high official in many Italian cities during the Middle Ages. Appointed by the people or their representatives, the podestà often exercised a supreme, despotic power; he had the ability to make peace and war, and to intervene in affairs both domestic and foreign. To avoid the clash of rival families so common in Italian civic affairs of the period, outsiders were commonly selected for the post. Venetians were in special demand, at least during the twelfth and thirteenth centuries, because common wisdom held that they were less concerned than other Italians in the politics of the mainland. Pisa's podestà Morosini, a Venetian, provides just such an example.

†Count Ugolino might well have preferred to die at Meloria than face the death which awaited him four years later. Having conspired with the Florentine Guelphs, yielded territory to Lucca, and neglected to negotiate the release of the Pisan prisoners in Genoa, he, along with two sons and two grandsons, were cast into the Tower of the Seven Streets in Pisa and left to starve, a harrowing incident immortalized by Dante in the *Divine Comedy.*

Now, with its naval strength shattered—never to be recovered—and with it its commercial lifelines crippled, Pisa lay vulnerable and weak. Soon enough, Florence, Lucca, and Genoa were attacking Pisa in concert by land and by sea. In 1292, they assaulted the port, took its defensive towers, and put the city to siege. When Pisa finally relented the following year, it was forced to accept grievous terms: all members of the Guelph League were exempt from levies and duties in Pisa and its territories, while Genoa took control of Corsica and a portion of Sardinia and was freed of any taxes on Elba. In addition, the Genoese were paid a ransom of 160,000 lire for their Pisan prisoners, even though fewer than half of the original eleven thousand captives were still alive after nearly a decade in the infernal dungeons of Genoa. The bells of all Pisan campaniles tolled in mourning, and the works on the Camposanto were redoubled so as to accommodate the multitude of dead.

Yet while Pisa had been stripped of much of its power, the city and its monuments had been spared pillage and the torch, and its artistic talent was intact. Indeed, at the height of the republic's misfortunes, Pisan art flourished. In the Campo dei Miracoli, Giovanni Cimabue, Giotto's master, was creating a colossal mosaic, *Christ in Glory Between the Virgin and John the Evangelist,* for the apse of the duomo. The baptistery, meanwhile, was being crowned by a dome and would soon be completed. Work on the Camposanto as well was going full tilt. There was even talk of finishing the campanile—but also a good many voices in favor of dismantling the misbegotten thing. In response, the Opera della Primaziale insisted on calling a commission, the first of a total of seventeen which would convene over the centuries, to assess the tower's state and stability. Two *magistri lapidum,* or master masons—Giovanni Pisano and Guido, the son of Giovanni di Simone—and Orsello, a *magister lignaminis,* or master carpenter, were tapped to do the honors.

On March 15, 1298, the three commission members, accompanied by a notary from the Opera della Primaziale and observed by a throng, ascended the spiral staircase of the campanile. Then, from the vertiginous heights of the seventh cornice, they used the most precise instrument that medieval engineering afforded, a *filo a piombo,* or plumb line, to measure and calculate the tower's degree of incline. By dropping weighted lines from the top of the campanile groundward on both the interior and exterior, and duly marking where the weights touched the walls, Pisano and company could determine the structure's variance from the perpendicular. Chances are that they did in fact make such calculations, yet among all of the notary's documentation of the commission's measurements—which still survives—no mention is made of the degree to which the tower tilted. Nor is there any reference to concerns about the campanile's stability. Indeed, the first commission seems to have taken the whole issue of the campanile's tilt very much in stride, a circumstance owing, surely at least in part, to the scores of other structures, particularly towers, all over Pisa and its environs that were also forever teetering on account of the *terreni limosi*.

At the same time, however, it is impossible to imagine that Giovanni Pisano, or any other master builder or mason around the Campo dei Miracoli, was not aware of the campanile's incorrigible flaw, that is to say, its excessive weight. Atop an insufficient foundation rose a mass of stone that exerted an incalculable load on the soft, unstable terrain. Had the tower *not* shifted, it would have been a miracle, but just how it would continue to react was anyone's guess. The commission may well have concluded that further construction would be ill-advised, or then again, the continued suspension of work on the tower may have been related solely to the desperate climate in beleaguered Pisa at the time. Whatever the case, well over a century after its founding, the campanile still had no belfry, and thus no true purpose.

Perhaps it was better that Giovanni Pisano did not get too drawn into the fickle workings of the tower, for his genius clearly lay elsewhere in the Campo dei Miracoli. His father was the artist Nicola Pisano, creator of the pulpit in Deotisalvi's Pisan baptistery as well as the pulpit in Siena's cathedral, among other works, and arguably the first genuine Renaissance sculptor. He was trained in southern Italy, in one of the artist workshops patronized by Frederick II, the Holy Roman emperor who sought to revive something of ancient grandeur with a brilliant, if short-lived, court culture known as *stupor mundi,* or "wonder of the world." In that milieu, the elder Pisano helped to resurrect the long-eclipsed ideals of classical sculpture after centuries of medieval inexactitude. When Pisano appeared in Tuscany around the middle of the thirteenth century (he was not born in Pisa), he brought his classical inclinations with him, and found not only a receptive audience for his ideas in the Campo dei Miracoli, but also no small fount of inspiration. In Giorgio Vasari's *Delle vite de' più eccellenti pittori, scultori, e architettori* (On the Lives of the Most Excellent Painters, Sculptors, and Architects), published in 1550, the artist-author points to a curious source of Nicola Pisano's Pisan artistic awakening:

> [A]mong the spoils brought back by the Pisan fleet were many marble pieces, including some ancient sarcophagi now in the Camposanto, among them, an especially beautiful one, portraying the Chase of Meleander after the Calydonian Boar. . . . Nicola, deeming it a very good piece, and being so pleased with it, applied himself industriously to reproduce its fashion, and that of other worthy sculptures that were on those other ancient sarcophagi, with such good results that after a very short time he came to be judged the best sculptor of his day. . . .

Giovanni Pisano carried on his father's efforts to render human forms, actions, and emotions in the classical manner, eschewing medieval rigidity for a nascent Renaissance humanism. In the works of both father and son, man as individual occupies a central place, and it is this peculiarly Renaissance sensibility that imbues their sculpture with its revolutionary character. For although the Pisanos' work was concurrent with the French Gothic school that was so much in vogue in western Europe, the two styles are worlds apart. The gaunt, elongated saints of the west façade of Chartres, for example, are serene and exquisite in their way, but they are mere types, symbols devoid of humanity or individuality and clearly not of this world. Not so the figures of the Pisanos. Giovanni's circular, marble pulpit in the Pisa cathedral bears a whole panoply of biblical scenes in deeply carved relief, and while the themes—the Annunciation, the birth of St. John the Baptist, the Nativity, the Adoration of the Magi, the Flight into Egypt, the Slaughter of the Innocents, the Betrayal, the Passion, the Crucifixion, and the Elected and the Damned—were all standard biblical fare familiar to all the faithful, Giovanni's expressionistic style brought the scenes miraculously to life. The countenances of his figures display the whole range of human emotions: joy and terror, ecstasy and torment, melancholy and wonder, sloth and vigor, the same as could be found etched on the faces of ordinary Pisans in the street.

Not that this humanizing impulse of the Pisanos and

their circle was always embraced by other artists working in the Campo dei Miracoli, however. At the same time that Giovanni was sculpting his pulpit in the duomo, Giovanni Cimabue, the master of Giotto and probably the most celebrated artist of the day, was creating the mosaic for the cathedral apse, but there is little that is innovative or stylistically groundbreaking in the latter's work. His mosaic depicts the great Pantocrator, or All Powerful, bestowing his blessing and holding in his left hand a book inscribed "I AM THE LIGHT OF THE WORLD," from the Gospel of St. John. Both the theme and the composition of the work follow orthodox, centuries-old Byzantine models, similar examples of which could be found in mosaics and murals all over the Christian world. Cimabue executed a grand work, undoubtedly, but it was scarcely his own, and compared to the vitality of Giovanni Pisano's pulpit, the mannered mosaic seems hollow and uninspired.

It is no coincidence that Nicola and Giovanni Pisano's humanizing works also helped to influence a change in the artist's place in European society as the Middle Ages gave way to the Renaissance. The Pisans were no anonymous artisans who took their cues from the books of *exempla*—the guidebooks so popular in the twelfth and thirteenth centuries that provided schematic models of architectural and artistic details for artisans and craftsmen to follow and helped to foster a remarkable degree of architectural unity across Europe and the Mediterranean. Their creations were bold and visionary, and they knew it and proclaimed it. On the pulpit of San Andrea in Pistoia, for example, Giovanni Pisano chiseled a telling testament: "Sculpted by Giovanni, who never produced unworthy works, born of Nicola, but endowed with better science, and more skill than was ever seen."

Beyónd the magnificent confines of the Campo dei Miracoli, though, the prospects for Pisa weren't nearly so bright. In addition to its commercial and territorial losses, Pisa now began to suffer from internal political turmoil and civil strife that would lay waste much of the political freedom at the heart of the republic. In 1312, the Holy Roman emperor Henry VII descended upon Italy intent on reviving imperial authority in the face of unrelenting Guelph-Ghibelline violence, the open hostility of Florence and Naples, and an increasingly defiant papacy under Clement V. In Ghibelline Pisa, Henry was greeted as a liberator, but he claimed to favor neither Guelphs nor Ghibellines, and proclaimed instead the authority of the Empire over all, *cuncta absoluto complectens Imperio.* Setting up a temporary court and base at Pisa, Henry heard the local grievances and did battle with Florence, and for a moment, at least, Pisa's spirits rose. A year after Henry and his troops marched into Italy, however, the emperor suddenly and mysteriously died—the victim, according to legend, of poison given to him in the sacramental wine by a Dominican friar. He was buried in the duomo at Pisa, in a tomb sculpted by Tino di Camaino, a former student of Nicola Pisano.

Into the vacuum created by Henry's death stepped one of his imperial lieutenants, Uguccione della Faggiola, a soldier, adventurer, and renowned Ghibelline chief. Convincing the Pisans that what they needed was a firm hand to restore their fortunes, he managed to get himself appointed not only podestà, but also *capitano del popolo,* or captain of the people, and thus assumed two positions originally conceived to keep each other in check. Now the de facto lord of Pisa, Uguccione hardly disappointed in fulfilling his promise to exercise a firm hand. For although Pisan troops under his command captured Lucca and defeated the Florentines and their allies from Naples at Montecatini in 1315, he also unleashed such a tyranny in Pisa that he was finally driven out of the city by a mob in 1316. A legion of lords and petty tyrants followed, among them Castruccio Castracane, to whom Niccolò Machiavelli dedicated a rather romanticized biography, and soon Pisan freedom was irretrievably lost and with it the true foundation of the republic. On occasion, the city would muster the troops, or hire a mercenary force, and win a battle, or regain a fraction of lost territory, but nothing could stem the decline.

Considering how Pisa was faced with the greatest possible calamities throughout the whole of the fourteenth century, not the least of which were the permanent loss of her fleet, resounding defeats on the battlefield, the emergence of Florence as her preeminent foe, virtual civil war inside the city walls, and plague, it is astonishing that work in the

Campo dei Miracoli never came to a standstill. No matter who was in power, the Opera della Primaziale managed to stay above the fray and kept the Campo dei Miracoli from becoming disputed—or quiet—ground. In some of Pisa's darkest hours, for instance, Taddeo Gaddi and Andrea Orcagna were busy painting frescoes in the Camposanto. Then, sometime around 1350, in the wake of the Black Death, Tommaso d'Andrea was entrusted with at last giving the campanile the one element it so conspicuously lacked: a belfry.

After a hiatus of approximately eighty years and more than a half century since Giovanni Pisano and the first commission took their measurements, the tower had settled sufficiently into the terrain to renew construction, or so must have thought Tommaso d'Andrea. As it stands, no extant documents record the campanile's final phase of construction or when exactly it took place. One of the few shreds of documentary evidence from this period can be found, curiously enough, on a wall of the Camposanto. In a fresco depicting the funerary procession of San Ranieri, patron saint of Pisa, painted by Antonio Veneziano between 1384 and 1386, the campanile is shown complete with belfry, and noticeably askew.

Tommaso d'Andrea was a child of the Campo dei Miracoli. His father, Andrea Pisano, had studied under Giovanni Pisano (no relation), and had worked on both the Camposanto and the late-Gothic church of Santa Maria della Spina on the Arno; his brother Nino, also a sculptor and architect, was especially sought after for his statues of the Madonna and Child. So once again, a native son would intervene in the saga of the campanile, and like the good progeny that he was, Tommaso carried on the architectural dictates of the Pisan Romanesque as set down by Buscheto di Giovanni Guidice three centuries earlier. Indeed, with seven stories already complete, anything else would have looked absurd.

Cylindrical in plan, like the rest of the tower, the belfry is smaller than the preceding orders. Its alternating bands of white and gray marble and its columns, rounded arches, and sculpted cornices are all in keeping with the stylistic precedents of the Campo dei Miracoli. Tommaso did, however, make one innovation. In *his* contribution to correcting, or at least accommodating, the tower's axis, Tommaso utilized a simple measure common in Pisa: he built a level belfry floor and accounted for the tilt by varying the steps needed to reach it from six on the south side, to only four steps on the north. Bells were hung in the open arches, and on the day the campanile was finished, nearly two hundred years after ground was first broken in 1173, the air filled with a peal the likes of which Pisans had never heard.

With the completion of the campanile, the landscape of the Campo dei Miracoli was nearly complete (the cathedral was finished in 1250, the hospital in 1258, and the baptistery in 1300; only the Camposanto would remain unfinished until 1465). Inside this sublime geography, Pisans found a metaphor for life: in the baptistery they were christened, in the duomo they were married, in the campanile they assumed a civic duty by gathering to watch the local pageantry, in the hospital they found succor, and in the Camposanto they were buried. No other medieval architectural conjunction could match the monuments of the Campo dei Miracoli in their scope, and few in their beauty, but there was also something unmistakably tragic about this square: nothing of what had made Pisa great, nothing of the splendor that they were to honor, had survived to see their completion. The city had lost its fleet, its commercial prowess, its political freedom, and its status as a republic. In the end, Pisa was reduced to mere merchandise to be bought and sold, a pawn. In 1399, Gherardo d'Appiano, the dissolute son of the last of Pisa's lords, sold the city to the Visconti of Milan for 200,000 florins; six years later, Pisa was sold again, this time to Florence. When the Florentines arrived to take possession of their new domain, one of the first measures they took was to seal the gate in the Campo dei Miracoli that allowed Pisans to walk directly past their bell tower—lest a sense of *campanilismo* should turn to defiance.

SIX

The Stuff of Myth

And then, to the dismay of all the philosophers, very many conclusions of Aristotle were by him [Galileo] proved false through experiments and solid demonstrations and discourses, conclusions which up to then had been held for absolutely clear and indubitable; as, among others, that the velocity of moving bodies of the same material, of unequal weight, moving through the same medium, did *not* mutually preserve the proportion of their weight as taught by Aristotle, but all moved at the same speed; demonstrating this with repeated experiments from the height of the Campanile of Pisa in the presence of the other teachers and philosophers, and the whole assembly of students.

—Vincenzo Viviani, *Racconto istorico della vita del Sigr. Galileo Galilei* (commonly known as *Vita di Galileo*) (1654)

When in 1639 Vincenzo Viviani arrived at *Il Giojello* ("The Little Jewel"), Galileo's villa in Arcetri outside of Florence, he was a young man of seventeen with little means, but a prodigious mind for mathematics and the crucial patronage of Ferdinand II, grand duke of Tuscany. Galileo was by then aged, infirm, nearly totally blind, and living the interior exile imposed by the Inquisition in 1633 for being "vehemently suspected of heresy."* The master was still lucid, however, and desperately in need of a secretary-scribe. Recognizing this, his inquisitors lifted the strict seclusion to which he had been sentenced in order to admit Viviani. For three years, Galileo rambled and recited as Viviani furiously took down everything—correspondence, dialogues, mathematical problems, physical theories, discourses, and, all the while, the recollections of a long life marked by equal measures of triumph and humiliation.

By all accounts, Viviani was as exemplary and devoted a disciple as any master could hope to find, and not just during those few years by Galileo's side. For although Viviani would go on to achieve considerable fame in his own right, becoming court mathematician to the grand duke of Tuscany and publishing a good many competent, if less than pioneering, works on geometry, throughout his life he dedicated much of his energies to vindicating his mentor's name and propagating Galilean scientific theories. It was Viviani who edited the first collection of Galileo's works and wrote the first biography of the astronomer, mathematician, and physicist, the *Vita di Galileo,* which became

---

*Galileo was condemned of heresy in 1633 by the tribunal of the Inquisition in the basilica of Santa Maria Sopra Minerva in Rome. The charge arose from Galileo's defense of the Copernican theory of the solar system which he published in *The Dialogue Concerning the Two Chief World Systems,* Florence, 1632.

something of a best-seller throughout Europe. Moreover, Viviani was the driving force behind Leopold de' Medici's establishment of the Accademia del Cimento, a scientific institution dedicated to experimenting with the theories of the late, great master, in Florence in 1657. The ever-grateful Viviani even left money in his will for the construction of a sepulchral monument to Galileo in Florence's church of Santa Croce, to place Galileo alongside Michelangelo, Machiavelli, and Leonardo Bruni. And finally, and not least significantly, it was Vincenzo Viviani who first placed Galileo atop the Tower of Pisa, a place where he would remain more or less fixed, at least in the collective Western imagination, for centuries to come—this despite the fact that in none of Galileo's writings, nor any of his personal correspondence, is the Pisan campanile mentioned, never mind anything about conducting a single experiment from its heights. Nor, for that matter, did any of the other "teachers and philosophers, and the whole assembly of students" from the university of Pisa whom Viviani places there have anything at all to say on the matter. Perhaps the only plausible explanation for such resounding silence about Galileo's groundbreaking, and quite public, scientific discovery at the tower—here, after all, was a lone genius shattering an Aristotelian dictum honored for millennia, all before a veritable throng, and, what's more, "with repeated experiments"—is that the events, quite simply, never took place. In all likelihood, the timeworn and assiduously reported image of Galileo dropping objects from the summit of the Tower of Pisa is the stuff of pure, unadulterated myth, all thanks, it seems, to the overly ripe imagination of an adoring disciple.

Galileo Galilei was born in Pisa on February 15, 1564, the first-born son of Vincenzo Galilei, a composer, music teacher, accomplished lutenist, and occasional wool trader, and Giulia Ammannati. The Galileis were a noble Florentine family of some note that had flourished with the Florentine republic—they had given the city a gonfalonier and numerous consuls—and declined precipitously with its fall. Upon marrying Giulia, who also descended from enfeebled nobility, Vincenzo Galilei settled in Pisa; the house where they lived, and where Galileo and a legion of siblings were born, still stands, modest and unassuming, on the via Giuseppe Giusti. To move from Florence to Pisa, mind you, was an unequivocal indication of a reversal of fortunes. By the mid-sixteenth century, anyone who had known Pisa at the height of its powers would scarcely have recognized the place. Pisa was no longer the powerful capital of an independent republic, but rather a sad and desolate port with a population of fewer than nine thousand. Far from deciding its own destiny, Pisa now labored under the Florentine yoke and the

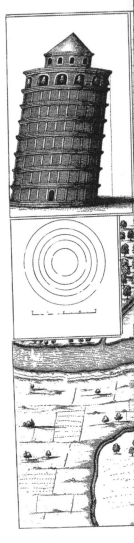

Pisa, 1695

TILT 99

decrees of a distant grand duke. The Arno, the river where its proud fleets once anchored, had long since silted up and was fit for little more than fishing vessels, while the canals around the city were stagnant and fetid. The merchandise moving in the market was mostly human slaves from Africa brought to work in the houses and estates of the rich, and in the palaces along the riverfront Lung' Arno, a few beleaguered noblemen hung on to delusions of past grandeur and tried to check their dwindling assets. Everyone with talent, connections, influence, or cunning had flocked to Florence, and Pisa was left with the dank air of a back-water.

Vincenzo Galilei established a school of music in the townhouse of a noble family named Bocca and made occasional forays to the wool exchange. His son, Galileo, meanwhile, grew up in an atmosphere of general domestic chaos and perpetually strained funds. Apart from a penchant for building his own clever toys, though, young Galileo's childhood in Pisa seems to have been altogether uneventful. Vincenzo, however, had ambitions for his son. In 1574, the family moved to Florence, and soon after, Galileo was enrolled in the prestigious school at the mountaintop abbey of Vallombrosa, twenty miles east of the city. He seemed to take to the rigors and austerity of the abbey exceedingly well, and in his fourth year, at the tender age of fifteen, he proclaimed his intention to take the cloth and become a monk. His father's reaction was swift and unambiguous: Galileo was promptly withdrawn from Vallombrosa. Piety was all very well and good, Vincenzo told his son, but his future did not lie in a cloister.

In the autumn of 1581, Galileo was back in Pisa, enrolled, according to his father's wish, in the university's medical school. This marked the beginning of an extraordinary intellectual awakening in Galileo, albeit one due less to the routine of his medical studies than to his discovery of complex mathematics at the hand of Ostilio Ricci, the court mathematician of the grand duke Francesco de' Medici, who was lecturing at Pisa. Soon enough, Galileo exchanged Hippocrates, Galen, and Avicenna for Euclid and Archimedes, and fast became Ricci's protégé—all to the considerable dismay of Vincenzo Galilei, who had rather hoped that his son would take up the more lucrative calling of medicine. To the elder Galilei, mathematics seemed too abstract, impractical, and undistinguished; on top of that, it paid poorly. Vincenzo's preoccupation with money was understandable since he plainly had none, a fact which his son would soon comprehend only too well: in 1585, Galileo's studies were suddenly cut short for lack of funds, and he was forced to return to Florence without a degree. The absence of academic credentials, however, appeared to matter little to Galileo, or at least it did nothing to check his progress. Shortly after leaving the university at Pisa, he was lecturing to the august Florentine Academy on the precise dimensions of Dante's *Inferno* (just the sort of intellectual gymnastics which Galileo relished), as well as inventing a hydrostatic balance, working out the practical applications of the pendulum, and writing a treatise on the center of gravity in solids, so influential that it would earn him acclaim as the Archimedes of his time. As fate would have it, this latter work also won him the respectable, if less than munificent, post of mathematical lecturer back at the Pisan university.

Galileo taught at Pisa from 1589 to 1591, precisely the years in which he is purported to have conducted his experiments from the Tower of Pisa—at least according to Vincenzo Viviani and nearly every Galilean biographer since. In the standard telling of this decisive chapter in the Galilean hagiography, Galileo is depicted as being at intractable odds with his Aristotelian colleagues on the university faculty. Cast as the impetuous young professor rebelling against the bigoted and narrow certainties left unquestioned since antiquity, Galileo represents the new science, the Copernican as opposed to the Ptolemaic view of the universe and the power of knowledge and logic over that of faith and dogma. In the face of it all, wrote Viviani evocatively, "He upheld the dignity of his professional chair with so great fame and reputation, before judges well-disposed and sincere, that many philosophers, his rivals, stirred with envy, were aroused against him." Finally, like a misunderstood prophet, he is driven from the university by a combination of ignorance and envy.

A less impassioned examination of Galileo's professional stint at Pisa reveals nothing to lend credence to the tale of his experiments from the campanile or the supposed clash with his Aristotelian colleagues. In fact, Galileo Galilei, the young professor, seems to have gone almost wholly unnoticed at Pisa. He published nothing while a professor at the university and left no record whatsoever of any public experiments or polemics with the other professors. One can only assume that Galileo dutifully taught the curriculum of Pythagoras, Euclid, Archimedes, and Leon Battista Alberti, and displayed a junior professor's obligatory deference toward his senior colleagues. If he believed any theory so earth-shattering as the Copernican view of the universe, he certainly did not express it at Pisa. So, after three rather uneventful years of teaching at the university, Galileo simply did not have his contract renewed.

Fortunately, a better-paid post came up at the university of Padua, where Galileo would remain for eighteen years and enjoy both inspiration and prosperity. It was there that he invented the proportional compass, or sector; the first crude, but effective, thermometer; and his version of a telescope.* His lectures were highly popular and attended not only by his formal students, but by visiting scholars, travelers, and personages from all over Europe. During his stint at Padua, Galileo's contract was renewed on three occasions, and his salary rose steadily from 180 to 1,000 florins per year. Padua deserves the credit for providing Galileo

---

*The invention of the first practical telescope was the work of two Dutch opticians, Johannes Lippershey and Zacharias Jansen, not Galileo, as often and erroneously stated.

with the ways and means for his intellect to soar. Through no fault of its own, perhaps, the sad fact is that Pisa failed to recognize the genius native son who had been in its midst.

Between an aged Galileo and an ingenuous Vincenzo Viviani, it is impossible to determine with certainty who conjured up the myth of the public experiments from the Tower of Pisa. Galileo was already seventy-five years old and racked by ill health when Viviani began to transcribe the master's recollections at Arcetri. He was under house arrest (although such illustrious visitors as the poet John Milton and the philosopher Thomas Hobbes did manage to steal in to see the great man) and sworn to a vow of silence, at least regarding cosmological theories, and he had been forced to recant his Copernican beliefs, under threat of torture and the stake, in a humiliating public trial in Rome. Galileo, so notoriously combative, was a beaten man, alone and embittered, and he may well have looked back on his years as a young professor with a less than objective gaze and inflated his own accomplishments for posterity's sake. Otherwise, it would seem more than odd that Galileo should have waited some fifty years to mention anything about events that marked a monumental scientific breakthrough and were purported to have been public spectacles to boot. Galileo did, in fact, refer to falling bodies and question Aristotle in his *Dialogues Concerning Two New Sciences,* but that work was published in 1638, near the end of his life and a year before Viviani appeared on the scene, and no reference is made, oblique or otherwise, to the Tower of Pisa: "Aristotle says that 'an iron ball of one hundred pounds, falling from a height of one hundred cubits reaches the ground before a one-pound ball has fallen a single cubit.' I [Salviati, a speaker in the dialogue who represents Galileo] say that they arrive at the same time."

Alternatively, the only other possible source of the myth of Galileo at the campanile could have been Vincenzo Viviani, the unwavering follower and amateur biographer who wished to see Galileo absolved and his name glorified (and by association, one supposes, Viviani's own glorified as well). Writing more than sixty years after the alleged experiments and more than a decade after the death of Galileo, Viviani may have simply exaggerated his master's achievements at Pisa because the truth was decidedly less exalted. How, Viviani must have thought, to explain the paucity of Galileo's contribution at Pisa if his subject was a colossal genius? By shattering a hitherto indisputable Aristotelian theory and painting a vivid portrait of a scientist as a brilliant, misunderstood lot, that's how. Viviani's *Vita di Galileo* was a rare biography in that it treated the life not of an emperor, a statesman, an ecclesiastic, or even an artist, but rather a scientist and mathematician. The work was clearly more than a mere panegyric: Viviani went a step further, taking exceptional liberties with the facts and coloring Galileo's life and labors in order to arouse a passion not just for the man but for science. It worked. The book was an instant and immense success throughout Europe; Galileo's fame justly spread, albeit posthumously, and Viviani reaped a tidy profit.

Once Galileo had been placed at the summit of the Tower of Pisa by Vincenzo Viviani, there was no way to get him down; the image proved just too compelling. As a backdrop for an epochal experiment, the campanile was perfect. If the Tower of Pisa seemed to defy logic and the laws of nature, so too did Galileo's demonstrations defy ancient wisdom. The whole scenario had a kind of picture-book simplicity that enabled anyone to grasp a law of physics that is anything but simple. Just as parables and medieval religious tableaux sought to portray biblical scenes, miracles, and the heroic sacrifices of martyr-saints for the benefit of the mostly illiterate faithful, so would the tale and iconography of Galileo atop the campanile explain an enigma of science to a largely ignorant public more accustomed to the habits of faith.

Not surprisingly, the strength and longevity of this Galilean myth has proven as unshakable as any religious dogma. Still, it is hard to judge Vincenzo Viviani too harshly for the original fabrication, full as he was with adoration for his master and the power of poetic license. It is worth keeping in mind as well that the parameters of biography were far from clearly defined in the seventeenth century, when hagiographies were, by and large, the norm, and biographers tended to play fast and loose with the facts, depending on their own agendas. The truly guilty parties in the matter are the legions of biographers who have followed in Viviani's wake and treated the *Vita di Galileo* as if it were a critical and unfailing source. If these subsequent biographers had confined themselves to simply recounting what Viviani had set in motion, that would have been bad enough, but they too seemed to get caught up in the vast potential that the mythic scene provided. Like the dinner-party diversion of whispering an anecdote in one's neighbor's ear and having it repeated to each subsequent guest, before hearing the final, much-altered version, the myth of Galileo and the tower grew successively more elaborate and convoluted as time passed. Consider, for example, the following excerpt from *The Scientific Works of Galileo,* published in 1921 by J. J. Fahie, an important English biographer of Galileo:

> Aristotle had said that, if two different weights of the same material were let fall from the same height, the two would reach the ground in a period of time inversely proportional to their weights. Galileo maintained that save for an inconsiderable difference due to the disproportionate resistance of the air, they would fall in the same time. The Aristotelians ridiculed such "blasphemy," but Galileo determined to make his adversaries see the fact with their own eyes. One morning, before the assembled professors and students, he ascended the leaning tower, taking with him a 10 lb. shot and a 1 lb. shot. Balancing them

on the overhanging edge, he let them go together. Together they fell, and together they struck the ground.

In the years between Viviani and Fahie, the story accumulated a whole host of details not present in the original
Vita di Galileo. The Aristotelians, for instance, have
become bolder and are reputed to ridicule Galileo's "blas-
phemy"; the experiment takes place rather vaguely "one
morning"; and the young professor is described as climb-
ing the campanile with two cannonballs, "a 10 lb. shot and
a 1 lb. shot," to be used in the experiment—a clever new
detail apparently included to provide readers with a clearer
picture of just what is supposed to have been dropped. Evi-
dently, Fahie thought it unnecessary to mention, as did
Viviani, that Galileo conducted the experiments "repeat-
edly"; no doubt he reckoned that one resounding trial was
quite enough.

Another Englishman, one Henry Moore, a professor of
physics at King's College, University of London, invented
his own rather confused version of the tale for the soberly
titled *Textbook of Intermediate Physics,* published in 1923:

In his experiments on the acceleration of freely
falling bodies, Galileo enclosed equal weights of different materials in a number of exactly similar
boxes. In this way the resistance offered to the passage of the boxes through the air was the same in all
cases for equal speeds. The boxes, each containing a

different material, were dropped simultaneously from the top of the leaning tower of Pisa, and an attempt was made to detect any differences in the times at which they reached the ground.

So far as could be observed, the boxes all reached the ground simultaneously, irrespective of their contents . . .

Suddenly, the cannonballs have been exchanged for "a number of exactly similar boxes," but just how many Moore doesn't say. Nor does he mention what they contain, though he seems to have muddled the idea of experimenting with different weights with that of experimenting with distinct materials of equal weight. That the indeterminate number of boxes reached the ground simultaneously "so far as could be observed" betrays a hint of doubt or timidity on the author's part, as if he himself wasn't altogether sure of the theory. The public too has conspicuously disappeared—no envious professors, bigoted Aristotelians, or crowd of students make their way into Moore's rendition; in fact, Galileo might very well have been alone.

Lastly, let us examine a more contemporary take on the myth from James Reston's *Galileo: A Life,* from 1994. The excerpt is lengthy because, frankly, Reston painted such a prodigious picture, one that aptly illustrates the extent to which the fiction had taken on mythic proportions:

He [Galileo] climbed atop the tower of Pisa. The boldness of the idea was its obviousness, but no one before him had thought of it, or had dared to attempt it. The problem was to measure the rate of free-fall. What better place was there to conduct the experiment than this nearby monument to man's imperfections? . . .

Up the winding staircase he carried balls of different weights and sizes, of lead and ebony, perhaps even of gold and porphyry and copper. Later he would imagine the difference in the flight of a hen's egg versus that of a marble egg. As legend has it, he advertised his demonstrations widely, bringing out an excited throng of students and professors. Emerging expansively at the top amid the pilasters and precarious open arcading, he played to his crowd. He was greeted by a roar. The odd catcall punctuated the amused cheers, for most of the crowd undoubtedly hoped to witness a fiasco. There was something about the tower that seemed to attract freaks and exhibitionists. Who was this junior genius, this radical, to challenge not only the senior experts in the field but Aristotle himself? Perhaps he was like the hunchback who had supposedly built the tower to lean this way to flaunt his own deformity!

Galileo was unintimidated by the gaze of the experts below. He reveled in his boldness and scorned their pedantry. "These grand personages who set out to discover the great truth and never quite find it give me a pain," he scoffed. "They can't find it, because they're always looking in the wrong place." His contempt for the pedestrians was pronied. "A good doctor needs to be accompanied by at least thirty scholars," he jeered. "If unaccompanied, others will say, 'this is an ignorant man. Better that he be a friar. At least they go about in pairs like spinach and brooms.'"

He had entered into a world of his own, exhibiting the enormous confidence of an original mind. "If you're going to find the truth, you have to employ fantasy," he mused. "You have to play at invention and guess a little. When I'm looking for the truth, I always look for the opposite, because great good and great evil are always there together like chickens in the market." As the balls thudded simultaneously at the base of the tower, Aristotle's formula made a thud as well.

Now, Reston offers what might be called the Hollywood version of the Galilean myth, and it is decidedly a big-budget affair, complete with a cast of thousands, a gripping script more concerned with drama than the historical facts, loads of atmosphere, and, naturally, Galileo in the full-blown leading role. The author attributes declarations to Galileo that he either never made or certainly never uttered in the context of the tower; besides, who could have possibly heard him above the din of the crowd? Instead of mere cannonballs or prosaic boxes, we have balls of lead, ebony, gold, porphyry, and copper! The tower, meanwhile, has suddenly acquired pilasters. And the public roars, provides catcalls, and cheers—and Galileo plays to the crowd, even as "his contempt for the pedestrians was profound." He scoffs, jeers, and muses, and dispatches Aristotle with a thud.

All of Reston's theatrics would be innocent enough if it weren't for a phrase he employs at the start of the passage: "The boldness of the idea was its obviousness, but no one before him had thought of it, or had dared to attempt it." Reston, like Viviani and so many others, attributes the refutation of Aristotle's dictum to the young Galileo at the tower even though there is ample evidence that Galileo arrived at his conclusions only in *Dialogues Concerning Two New Sciences,* published in 1638 when he was an old man. In an earlier unpublished work entitled *De Motu,* Galileo had groped with the issue of motion, but he never managed to articulate or develop a full-fledged law. The true authorship of the theory of falling bodies belongs not in fact to Galileo, but rather to Girolamo Cardano (1501–1576), an Italian mathematician, physician, and astrologer who was the illegitimate son of Facio Cardano, a learned Milanese jurist and amateur mathematician. Also known as Jerome Cardan, Girolamo Cardano was a man of peculiarly diverse passions: he gained widespread renown for the publication of mathematical and scientific works such as *Practica arithmeticae generalis* and *De Subtil-itate Rerum,* but he also displayed a less-than-scientific penchant for astrology, inordinately deep belief in the power of dreams and omens, and an addiction to gambling. In addition, he fancied himself one of the world's five or six celebrated men who, like Socrates, was believed to possess a guardian demon. Like Galileo, Cardano taught at various Italian universities—he was a professor of medicine at Pavia and later at Bologna—and he too had his confrontations with the Inquisition. And even though not a household name today, he was not an obscure, unknown figure of his time. On the contrary, it is difficult to believe that Viviani, if not Galileo, was not aware of Cardano's achievements, among them the findings he presented in *Opus Novum de Proportionibus,* published in Basel in 1570:

> Two balls of the same material falling in air arrive at a plane at the same instant.
>
> It is assumed that they fall from the same point; for a proposition is not to be taken in an absurd sense unless by an invidious or ignorant critic. Let *a,* therefore, be triple the size of *b,* two balls alike of lead, iron, or stone of a given sort. I say that they will reach the plane *cd* in equal times.

One could scarcely be any clearer or more precise than Cardano on this fundamental law of motion, and yet he

has been largely ignored by history and robbed of his legit-
imate discovery. The recognition due Cardano may well
have been suppressed or at least underplayed by both scientific bodies and ecclesiastical powers because they
thought a scientist of illegitimate birth with an inordinate
interest in astrology and similar chicaneries was not an
example to uphold. On the other hand, Galileo may have
unjustly eclipsed Cardano due simply to the unstinting
efforts of Vincenzo Viviani and the unforgettable and
peerless setting provided by the Tower of Pisa.

SEVEN

Of Poets and Men of Progress

Within the surface of the fleeting river
The wrinkled image of the city lay,
Immovably unquiet, and forever
It trembles, but it never fades away . . .

—Percy Bysshe Shelley, "Evening: Ponte al Mare, Pisa" (1821)

In the spring of 1817, two English architects, Edward Cresy and George Ledwell Taylor, appeared in Pisa bearing the tools of the engraver's art, a well-thumbed edition of Vitruvius's *De architectura,* and an inextinguishable love for classical architecture and the ruins of the ancient world. Actually, the men were bound for Rome, but had stopped off at Pisa to visit the Campo dei Miracoli. Both Cresy and Taylor had studied the Pisan Romanesque at the Royal Academy of Arts in London, yet neither was quite prepared for the sensation of spatial exuberance which overcame them as they stood in the midst of the cathedral square for the first time. It wasn't the Colosseum or the imperial forums of Rome, it's true, but in scale and sheer architectural power, the conjunction of duomo, baptistery, Camposanto, and campanile was grander than anything that the two had seen on their continental travels. The Englishmen promptly decided to stay. The Eternal City, they thought, could wait.

In a period marked by architectural and archaeological rapacity, in which the so-called cultivated men of Europe took it upon themselves to plunder ancient sites of everything from mosaics to actual monuments, Cresy and Taylor merely wished to render what they encountered in fine copperplate engravings. Theirs would be the first systematic examination of the monuments in the Campo dei Miracoli; all would be drawn with every effort at technical mastery, to scale and with the utmost accuracy that line engraving would allow. There would be no concessions to fancy, as in the half-real, half-imaginary scenes of a Giovanni Battista Piranesi. In setting such parameters, Cresy and Taylor clearly saw their enterprise as much in a scientific as artistic light.

For the better part of a year, Cresy and Taylor set up camp in the Campo dei Miracoli. They measured the monuments from top to bottom and inside and out, they calculated the position and distance between each edifice in the square, and they worked out the proportions and scale that had been set down by Buscheto and followed by his successors. Only after taking these measurements did the men then begin to sketch the preliminary cartoons of the archi-

'*They were seen to fall evenly.*'

"*They were seen to fall evenly.*" Galileo making his experiments on the velocity of falling bodies.

tectural landscape from which they would ultimately etch the copperplates for their definitive renderings. The pair's style was sober, in contrast to the supreme artistry found in the works of Piranesi, Sir Robert Strange, or Claude Lorrain, but it had the virtue of being thoroughly unaffected. Cresy and Taylor produced dozens of engravings, many of which would subsequently appear in their *Architecture of the Middle Ages in Italy,* published in London in 1829; others were sold as prints to the burgeoning British middle class that was fueling a nineteenth-century engraving boom. In a matter of decades, photography would come to eclipse the engraver's art, and daguerreotypes, calotypes, and collodion prints would be all the rage, but in the early nineteenth century, these painstaking, finely etched scenes were still the closest that a distant observer could come to admiring the monuments of the Campo dei Miracoli.

Given their technical prowess, when Cresy and Taylor turned their attention to the tower, one cannot help but think that it was not without a certain degree of disdain. These were men of an enlightened, scientific bent, and as neoclassical architects, they were inspired by the order and precision of the ancients. Their affinity for the classically rooted Romanesque architecture of Pisa was natural, but it is unlikely that they saw any pathos in a skewed tower. If they could have righted the campanile, one suspects, they would have gladly done so—in the name of progress. As it was, the Englishmen confined themselves to measuring the tower with characteristic scrupulousness and producing engravings of the edifice both in full frontal position and in section, the latter image allowing an observer to appreciate for the first time the campanile's complex inner workings.

Among Cresy and Taylor's exhaustive measurements of the tower, of course, was a calculation of the structure's inclination, the fifth in the tower's history: Giovanni Pisano in 1298 was the first to take measurements; he was followed by Giorgio Vasari in 1550 and the architect Alessandro Da Morrona in 1787 and again in 1812. And although more than five hundred years and incalculable scientific and technological advances separated Giovanni Pisano from Cresy and Taylor, the instrument they used remained the same: the time-honored plum line. In keeping with all of their predecessors, the Englishmen conducted their measurements from the height of the seventh cornice, thus enabling them to make a comparative assessment of the campanile's movement with relative accuracy. The earliest record of the tower's tilt available to Cresy and Taylor dated from 1550, when Vasari calculated the inclination at *"sei braccia e mezzo,"* or "six and a half arms," which, converted to the metric system, comes to approximately 3.80 meters. Cresy and Taylor's figure of "12 feet 6¼ inches" renders 3.84 meters—which is to say that in nearly three centuries, the tower had scarcely moved at all. The news astonished everyone, except perhaps Alessandro Da Morrona, who had come to the same conclusion in 1812 and seen his findings largely ignored. Suddenly, a good number of architects and historians, among them

Ranieri Grassi, an eminent Pisan art historian, began to actively defend the theory that the campanile had been designed purposely askew. The brilliance of the tower, insisted Grassi, lay precisely in what he called its impression of *"d'istantanea rovina,"* or "imminent collapse." This distinction was an important one, as it transformed a flawed, misbegotten pile into a magnificent folly, a veritable wonder of the world. Naturally, most Pisans embraced the new, albeit thoroughly erroneous, interpretation as an emblem of their city's long-gone glory and prowess. Until then, the Tower of Pisa had been a largely local phenomenon, and a source of acute embarrassment. Now, however, word of the audacious, law-defying campanile spread, drawing the curious to gaze in awe and admire the ingenuity of its creators. In Great Britain, at least, Edward Cresy and George Taylor's exacting engravings soon gave the public an idea of just how skewed things could be abroad.

Hard on Cresy and Taylor's heels came Percy Bysshe Shelley, the arch-romantic poet, political and social rebel, and all-around enemy of established mores. Fleeing the social constraints of late-Georgian London, he and his second wife, Mary, sought inspiration amid the plentiful ancient ruins and relative comforts of Italy. They arrived in Pisa in May 1818, only to find, in the poet's words, a "large disagreeable city, almost without inhabitants." (Mary was kinder, terming Pisa merely a "quiet half-unpeopled town.") Despite the rather grim first impres-

View of Pisa, by David Roberts, 1859

sion, however, something about the provincial capital, with its glorious, half-crumbling monuments from a distant golden age, appealed to the poet's romantic sensibilities. He admired Andrea Orcagna's frescoes in the Camposanto, marveled at the incongruity of the tower, and came to find the climate and the Arno agreeable. Mary, by contrast, thought Pisa "a dull town" and was appalled to find "criminals condemned to labour publickly in the streets heavily ironed in pairs . . . you could get into no street but you heard the clanking of their chains." The Shelleys would continue on to Lucca, Leghorn, Rome, and Naples, but they returned to Pisa sporadically over the next few years, finally setting up house in town in early 1821, at the Tre Palazzi di Chiesa.

The poet was twenty-eight years old and Mary a tender twenty-three.

Following the Shelleys' lead, a clique of expatriates soon gravitated to Pisa. The illustrious group included Edward and Jane Williams, the poet Leigh Hunt, Captain Edward John Trelawny, the Irish writer and translator John Taaffe, and, light of them all, Lord Byron, with his mistress Teresa Gamba in tow. This Pisa Circle, as Trelawny dubbed them, was composed of progressive-minded couples with a romantic spirit and a collective desire to resist the restraints and artifices of the "old order." Never mind that with the exception of Teresa Gamba and her brother Pietro, there wasn't a Pisan, or even an Italian, among them. Pisa became a refuge, an exotic setting, in Shelley's words, a "Paradise of Exiles." In truth, it is hard to point to anything particularly paradisiacal about Pisa in the early nineteenth century, but from a romantic standpoint, the city did possess certain subtle charms. To begin with, Pisa was *not* a principal stop on the Grand Tour, something that Byron and Teresa Gamba appreciated because it enabled them to avoid, in the poet's words, the "gossip-loving" English who flocked to Florence, Venice, and Rome. From Pisa, Shelley, Byron, and Williams could also indulge their passion for sailing. And furthermore, palaces could be rented in Pisa for a song, and there were plenty of evocative ruins about from which to draw inspiration. Indeed, most of the town was ruinous; as Percy Shelley wrote in "The Tower of

Famine," they walked "Amid the desolation of a city, / Which was the cradle, and is now the grave / Of an extinguished people . . ."

Romanticism has been called, among other things, "the cult of the extinct," and the romantics were never better occupied than when scrambling about ancient ruins. The remains of Rome, Greece, and Etruria evoked images of some prelapsarian, heroic age that the poets and artists were eager to resurrect.* Granted, Pisa wasn't Rome, but there were ruins enough to help to conjure up the glories of the past and inspire sublime reverie. The monuments in the Campo dei Miracoli were already centuries old and thus sufficiently hoary to arouse the curiosity of the Pisa Circle. Shelley, Leigh Hunt, and Lord Byron especially were fond of visiting the Camposanto to examine Orcagna's *Triumph of Death;* they admired Nicola and Giovanni Pisano's pulpits in the baptistery and the duomo; and they gazed in wonder at the tower, which, at latest count, leaned twelve feet, six and a quarter inches askew. "Pisa with its hanging tower and Sophia-like dome remind me," said Byron, "of an eastern place."

The romantic vision of the Tower of Pisa couldn't have

*In this regard it is interesting to note that in his memorial portrait of Percy Bysshe Shelley, the painter Joseph Severn tellingly set the poet in a landscape replete with ruins. The canvas, entitled *Shelley Composing "Prometheus Unbound" in the Baths of Caracalla,* shows a surprisingly boyish rebel poet drawing inspiration from the Roman ruins for his dramatic poem on Prometheus's own revolt against the gods.

differed more profoundly from that of more scientifically inclined men like Edward Cresy and George Taylor. If, as one would suspect, the English architects had lamented the campanile's slanted state in the name of the classical ideals of order and symmetry, it was precisely the anomaly of the tower's tilt that the romantics embraced. That the campanile was singular, wondrous, irregular, brimming with pathos, and suggestive of "an eastern place" was, to the romantic sensibility, at least, cause for admiration and celebration. Indeed, one of romanticism's greatest contributions to aesthetics was its ethos that discovered beauty in unconventional places like a storm-tossed sea, a desolate heath, a ruin, or a crooked tower.

For all of their impact, however, the romantics' stay in Pisa was actually quite short. On July 8, 1822, Percy Bysshe Shelley and Edward Williams boarded the less-than-seaworthy *Don Juan* and set sail across the Gulf of Spezia. Edward Trelawny was there to see them off, along with a Genoese sailor who, as the boat slipped away, is said to have commented, "Look at those black lines and the dirty rags hanging on them out of the sky—they are a warning; look at the smoke on the water; the devil is brewing mischief." They were the last ones to see Shelley and Williams alive. The poet's body was washed ashore ten days later, Williams's soon followed. In a highly charged rite that no doubt would have pleased the poet, Lord Byron had the bodies cremated on the beach at Viareggio, north of Pisa. "We have been burning the bodies of Shelley and Williams on the seashore," he wrote to Margaret Jane King Moore, another member of the Pisa Circle. "You can have no idea what an extraordinary effect such a funeral pile has, on a desolate shore, with mountains in the background and the sea before, and the singular appearance the salt and frankincense gave to the flame."

Not surprisingly, the Pisa Circle soon broke up. Byron, Teresa Gamba, Mary Shelley, and Leigh Hunt and his family all moved on to Genoa, while Pisa reverted to its somnolent self. The legacy of the romantics, however, lingered on, and not just in the works composed by the Circle while there. Thanks in large part to these works—including much of Byron's *Don Juan* (cantos six through ten, at least); "Adonais," Percy Shelley's elegy on the death of Keats; and Mary Shelley's novel *Valperga: Or the Life and Adventures of Castruccio, Prince of Lucca*—and the posthumous fame of both Shelley and Byron (the latter died just two years after Shelley, fighting for Greek independence from the Ottoman empire), Pisa became a de rigueur stop on a romantic pilgrimage trail. Soon a steady stream of travelers, poets, students, and nonconformists of every stripe turned up to pay homage at the haunts where the Pisa Circle had lived and played in their Paradise of Exiles. One such pilgrim-traveler was the French poet and novelist Louise Colet, whose diary of her stay at Pisa provides an intimate glimpse of life in the town in the midnineteenth-century. A passage on her visit to the Tower of Pisa is particularly revealing, saying much about the evo-

lution of the tower and the shifting sentiments of
observers toward it:

I was anxious to climb this famous leaning tower
that now stood before me, graceful and weightless,
standing out against the blue sky with its eight cylindrical galleries of columns; but when I wanted them
to open the door to let me up, difficulties began. No
less than three people at a time are allowed up, I'm
told, since two travellers (likely lovers) jumped over
the rail at the top of the tower to commit suicide.

I call to my cab-driver and look for a third person
in the deserted square, but to no avail. While I
debate with the intransigent keeper, a cab arrives
delivering a visitor; the man joins us, and at length
we are allowed up. The tower is 184 ft. tall, and
completely sheathed in marble; the foot slips on the
smooth stone; giddiness overcomes one as you
progress between these open galleries and the eye is
dazzled by the intensity of the light on a summer
day, embracing the vast horizon that stretches out all
around; the body, as if attracted towards the
precipice, staggers through the space between the
columns; I am compelled to lean on the arm of my
accidental companion.

Once on the platform, an incommensurable
expanse is revealed to our eyes; the blue sea merges
with the sky to the south-west, and in this twofold

blue the little islands of Gorgona and Caprara emerge; further away, the uncertain lines of Corsica and Elba can be made out; on a closer plane, Livorno stands out right by the edge of the waves; following the coastline you can see the spot where Byron burned Shelley's body on the funeral pyre. . . .

I descend reluctantly, despite the queasiness which the seeming oscillation of the monument provokes in me. The tower feels unsteady to me, as if it would drag us along in its fall. It is a known fact that stretching a rope from its summit to the ground, on the leaning side, the top will extend over the base by over 9 ft. This inclination was used by Galileo in his experiments on the falling of heavy bodies.

There is a good deal to glean from Colet's account. On a tragic note, it seems that travelers (lovers?) were already turning to the Tower of Pisa as a suitably dramatic setting from which to leap to their deaths (a sadly persistent tradition). They were overcome, one presumes, with *le mal du siècle*, that wholly romantic malady consisting of more or less equal doses of the jadedness of Byron's Childe Harold, the revulsion of Châteaubriand's René, and the *weltschmerz* of Goethe's Werther. As could well be expected in such circumstances, the Pisan authorities were obliged to restrict access to the campanile (although it is hard to understand how the measure of allowing no less than three visitors at a time would help to prevent suicides). The change, however, was a significant one, for unlike the other monuments in the Campo dei Miracoli, entrance to the Tower of Pisa was no longer free and unimpeded. No one suggested barring visitors from the loggia of the baptistery or the upper galleries of the duomo, from whence one could easily plunge to one's death as well, because, frankly, it wasn't deemed necessary. Apparently, if the forlorn decided to exit this world at Pisa, they wanted to do it from the Leaning Tower.

In addition, Colet found the cathedral square deserted, which seems to indicate that Pisa had lost nothing of the desolate air described by the Shelleys upon their arrival. On the subject of the tower's claim to fame, Colet alluded to the technique used to determine the tower's inclination—although her figure of "9 feet" was wildly off the mark—and she perpetuated the Galilean myth. Thus, here, in the choices of what to include in her fleeting impression of the campanile, Louise Colet betrayed a uniquely nineteenth-century turn of mind that elevated the Tower of Pisa to the stature of an architectural and cultural icon, a station far above its function as a bell tower or its relative importance in the scheme of the Campo dei Miracoli.

The appearance of Cresy and Taylor, a circle of romantics, and the assorted travelers who followed in their wake provided evidence that perhaps Pisa was less a cultural backwater than many locals had come to accept it to be. Not only were these foreigners visiting Pisa and the

Print of the Leaning Tower of Pisa, mid-nineteenth century, by
G. Ciuti, Palazzo dell'Opera della Primaziale, Pisa, Italy

Campo dei Miracoli, but they were drawing it and writing about it, too. What Pisa needed, therefore, thought the civic-minded, was a bit of beautification and urban renewal, and nowhere more so than in the Campo dei Miracoli, the symbolic center of the city's former splendor. Over the centuries, corners of the cathedral square had been steadily usurped until, by the nineteenth century, there were market stalls crowded around the monumental Porta al Leone, maintenance sheds hard by the Camposanto, a latrine behind the duomo, and a warren of walled orchards literally pressing against the east side of the campanile. All of it would have to go. The square would be restored to look as it had originally been envisioned, with its four principal monuments rising pristine and unobstructed.

In 1838, the architect Alessandro della Gherardesca—a distant relative of the infamous Count Ugolino della Gherardesca, who in an earlier era had escaped capture at the Battle of Meloria and was later starved to death in a tower in Pisa for his crimes against the republic—was commissioned by the Opera della Primaziale to renovate the space around the exterior of the campanile. A professor of architecture at Pisa's Academy of Fine Arts, and a vigorous exponent of romantic, neo-Gothic architecture in Tuscany, Gherardesca at once saw his task as twofold. First, he would free the tower of superfluous clutter by eliminating both the high wall that separated it from the orchards to the east and a sixteenth-century balustrade that protected the periphery of the tower and opened to the square to the west. These unwanted, haphazard architectural elements, insisted the architect, prevented observers from approaching the tower and appreciating its beauty in all its dimensions. This, in turn, brought him to his second task, unearthing the column plinths and base of the campanile, which had become buried on the south side due to the settlement of the structure in the subsoil. Unless the Tower of Pisa was excavated and wholly exposed, he insisted, it would never attain its full aesthetic potential. For Gherardesca, the project was less a commission than a crusade, as he related in his account of his efforts, *Apéndice alle consideración sulla pendenza del Campanile della Cattedrale pisana,* "Miscellanée artistiche" *(Considerations on the Inclination of the Pisan Campanile),* Pisa, 1838:

> Thank God we are living in a period in which the desire to conserve the legacy of the glorious republic of our forefathers is very much alive. I am but a confirmation of this new enthusiasm, for I have been entrusted not only with the restoration of the tower, but also with the elimination of the superfluous elements which surround it, and the complete exposure of the ground floor and the base from which it rises, in order to capture the full prestige of so noble and illustrious a work.

Alas, Gherardesca's resounding enthusiasm was not matched by an equal measure of caution. His considerations were well-meaning enough, to be sure, but they were exclusively visual and aesthetic: he never seemed to worry that so aggressive and hasty an intervention might unsettle the delicate equilibrium which the tower had attained after centuries of shifting fate. And so, in due course, the orchard wall came down and so too the sixteenth-century balustrade. A walkway, or *catino,* was dug out around the periphery of the tower, and as the base and column plinths became exposed, one could clearly see that the foundation had indeed sunk into the ground on the south side. The Tower of Pisa had most definitely *not* been built askew, thus laying to rest a centuries-old quarrel—and immortalizing Alessandro della Gherardesca, who was alternately trumpeted as a hero or denounced as a spoiler, depending upon where one stood in the debate. As more terrain was excavated around the campanile, however, laborers suddenly struck ground beneath the water table and the whole catino flooded over. Works came to an abrupt halt, the tower was closed indefinitely, and Gherardesca was promptly relieved of his position as architect in charge of the campanile. Soon after, Bruno Scorzi, the ninety-second president of the Opera della Primaziale, called for a new commission, the second one in the tower's 667-year history, to evaluate the tower. Much to his humiliation,

Gherardesca was left out of the group. Rather than romantic types, the Opera had clearly opted for more technical minds; the commission was composed of a professor of trigonometry and two engineers—in short, men of progress.

EIGHT

The Tiltin' Hilton

"This is Abel George One. Fire!"

The order, nearly given, which would have brought down
   an Allied bombardment on the tower during the Italian
   campaign of World War II.

The Tower of Pisa limped into the twentieth century decrepit and abused, and suffering from exacerbated wounds, but its condition was no more dire than that of Italy as a whole. For Italians, the century dawned tragically with a regicide; in 1900, King Umberto I, widely known as Umberto the Good, was shot dead by an anarchist assassin at Monza. Only recently united, Italy scarcely had time to mourn, consumed as it was in a dizzying array of shifting cabinets, falling governments, riots, questionable military interventions at home and abroad, feudal land wars, political assassinations, and labor strikes, of which there were no less than six hundred in the first six months of 1901. Naturally, burdened with perpetual crises, a restive, irascible Parliament exhibited little interest in the precarious state of a medieval bell tower. Nothing short of a disaster would draw public and parliamentary attention to the fate of the Pisan campanile. As it happened, catastrophe wasn't long in coming.

In the spring of 1902, a fissure appeared in one of the lofty blind arcades on the northern face of the campanile of Venice's Piazza San Marco. That bell tower, begun precisely one thousand years before and altered in the early sixteenth century, had long been one of the most cherished and recognizable landmarks in the city, rising 320 feet in the piazza between the architectural mayhem of the basilica of San Marco and the orderly formalism of Vincenzo Scamozzi's Procuratie Nuovo. Upon examining the crack in the brick face, municipal architects and engineers determined that the damage was insignificant and could be addressed in the course of routine maintenance. By the summer, however, nothing had been done, even though the fissure had grown and small bits of brick and mortar were occasionally falling into the piazza. On July 11, the architects and engineers returned, and once again assured city officials that there was no imminent danger, and certainly no cause for alarm. Just to allay any misgivings, nevertheless, they installed a series of glass sensors throughout the tower to detect any undue movement in the structure. The following day, observers found that the pieces of brick raining down from the campanile had turned into a deluge and that the crack now was a gaping wound. When engineers arrived, their inspection revealed that most of the glass sensors that they had installed only the day before had shattered. Still, it was Saturday, and they determined that any further intervention could wait until Monday. No precautions were taken and the campanile and piazza remained open.

At 9:30 in the morning on Monday, July 14, a municipal engineer and a police inspector approached the tower and were shocked to discover that the campanile's fissure now ran from the ground level all the way to the height of the belfry. The floor of the piazza beneath the tower lay strewn with debris. The police inspector, if not the engineer, foresaw a potential disaster and ordered the tower, as well as all of the cafés and shops in the piazza, to be evacuated. With the public's mood at once panic-filled and strangely festive—some thought the whole episode a hoax—police eventually managed to clear the square of all but its pigeons. Everyone watched and waited. Then, at 9:47, the fissure burst open with the suddenness of a thunderclap, and amid screams and cries from the multitude, the campanile's massive pyramidal roof teetered to and fro; the slender columns of its belfry exploded, the bells issued some last discordant chimes; and the whole tower collapsed with a roar and disappeared in a billowing cloud of millennium-old dust. Some witnesses claimed to have seen the gilded angel from the campanile's apex escape the fall and ascend toward heaven. Remarkably, there were no fatalities or injuries, but nonetheless, one of Italy's most singular campaniles had been reduced to rubble, and that was tragedy enough.*

For Pisa, at least, there was something fortuitous about the fall of the San Marco campanile. If previously public opinion had remained steadfastly indifferent toward the state of the Tower of Pisa, many now took up its salvation as a kind of cause célèbre. No one wanted to see another collapsing campanile, least of all Italy's ministry of education, or, more specifically, the ministry's department of antiquities and fine arts, which did not want to be perceived as incapable of preserving its own cultural patrimony. There were, however, few parallels to be drawn between the two celebrated campaniles. True, both towers were potent symbols of formerly powerful rival maritime republics, and both were roughly contemporaneous, but there the similarities ceased. The Venetian campanile was square in ground plan and built of brick; and unlike the Pisan tower's eight levels of open arches, each face was divided into four recessed blind arcades that rose from the ground to the belfry story. Finally, atop the belfry in Venice sat a weighty masonry frieze crowned by a pyramidal roof with an angel at its point. The tower, intact, looked nothing if not thoroughly robust, especially when compared to the open, delicately balanced plan of the Pisan campanile. Structurally, the edifices were radically differ-

---

*A reconstructed campanile, slightly altered and repositioned in the Piazza San Marco, was inaugurated in 1912.

ent—one, an almost seamless mass of brick; the other, an airy column of columns—and few if any would have ever guessed that the former would collapse and the latter would survive. As for the ground beneath the two campaniles, indeed beneath the two cities, Venice is built on a lagoon and Pisa a bog. Thus, it was generally assumed that the ground beneath the campanile of San Marco had given way, causing the fissure and the subsequent ruin. Yet when the rubble had been cleared from the piazza, investigators were astonished to discover that the tower's pile foundations were in excellent condition and in firm ground. Further investigation revealed that the principal cause of the structural failure was the excessive weight of the tower's sixteenth-century additions—new belfry, frieze, and roof—on its already aged brick. There hadn't been any original, inextricable flaw in the structure of the tower; its ailments stemmed from later alterations and additions, none of them delicate. In the end, the Venetian campanile succumbed to a combination of abuse and neglect, and the whole debacle read like a cautionary tale on the fragility of the architectural landscape and man's capacity to preserve or to spoil it.

So, the campanile's collapse in Venice was enough to win from the ministry what Pisan officials had for years been pleading for, namely, a new commission to analyze and remedy *their* campanile. In 1907, the third commission in the Tower of Pisa's 734-year history set to work, and although its mandate was essentially no different from that of Giovanni Pisano in 1298, this time, commission members assured the public, the advances of the twentieth century would cure the ailing campanile. The group tapped to save the tower was, once again, exclusively Pisan, mostly engineers and geologists from the University of Pisa, but also a municipal architect as well as a representative each of the Opera della Primaziale and the archbishop.

For three years the commission members scrupulously gathered data; they evaluated the tower's movement, took soil samples, measured the foundation, and tried, in vain, to stanch the flow of water persistently flooding the base of the tower. As their investigations proceeded, however, the group grew progressively less sanguine and their prognoses less rosy. When in 1910 it finally came time to present their conclusions, the committee members were unanimously gloomy. Worst among their findings was that the campanile was still slowly, but implacably, on the move. Using the hundred-year-old measurements of Edward Cresy and George Ledwell Taylor as a benchmark, commission member Paolo Pizzetti, a geodesist from the University of Pisa, calculated that the campanile had moved an additional 20 centimeters in less than a century, bringing its variance from the perpendicular to a full 4.04 meters. In addition, the water emerging from the foundation was bringing with it soil and mineral deposits, thus further undermining the *terreni limosi.* Another earthquake on par with that of 1846, or, worse still, another aggressive "restoration" like the one undertaken in 1838 by

Alessandro della Gherardesca, could well signal the end of the campanile, agreed the distinguished commission members.

As for solutions to the tower's chronic ills, well, the great scientific minds of Pisa were generally at a loss. Some proposed filling in Gherardesca's catino with cement in order to stop the flow of water and halt the tower's slow decline, but it was unlikely that this decidedly regressive measure would achieve either end. Others thought it wise to close the tower to the public, some going so far as to recommend cordoning off the whole corner of the Campo dei Miracoli where the tower stood. Finally, the third commission, the same one that had promised foolproof twentieth-century results only three years before, agreed to the only measure it could think up that would both show the public and the education minister, the press and the archbishop, a certain degree of resolve and at the same time not unduly imperil the campanile: they silenced the bells. "As a security precaution of the utmost prudence, and unless any pertinent studies deem otherwise," went the commission report, "it is recommended that the ringing of the bells, and with it their pendular movement, should cease." So now the Tower of Pisa was no longer just lame, but mute too.

For all the dashed hopes of the third commission, no one need have worried that it would be the Tower of Pisa's last. Commissions dedicated to the tower's preservation and well-being were almost constantly at work through the first half of the twentieth century. Another promptly formed in 1912, for instance, and after a hiatus for World War I, others followed in 1924, 1925, 1926 (two, in fact), 1927, and 1932. Invariably the commissions' mandates were the same—secure the tower!—but so too were their inevitable failures. On occasion, some maintenance was deemed necessary, and a column, arch, or plinth would be restored or an ashlar block replaced, but otherwise, nothing really changed at the campanile except its inclination, which progressed nicely.

Outside the Campo dei Miracoli, however, the scene was anything but idle. By the early decades of the twentieth century, Pisa was no longer the somnolent backwater or "paradise of exiles" that the romantics had found so endearing. Sadly, the city had long since turned its back on the sea; industrialization had brought cotton mills, foundries, the vast St. Gobain glassworks, and, uncompromising socialist and anarchist convictions. Much of what plagued Italy, including strikes, riots, political violence, and institutionalized corruption, could be found in its just proportion in Pisa. Not even the city's landmarks were considered safe from strife. A widespread fear among Pisan authorities of the era was that anarchist provocateurs would try to topple the campanile. Starting around the turn of the century, police regularly patrolled the Campo dei Miracoli. Meanwhile, pitched battles between leftist groups and Fascists were common enough in the streets and piazzas, and death squads too, like the one that in 1921 put a bullet in the head of Carlo Cammeo, a teacher and local socialist leader. Then, in 1922, Benito Mussolini marched on Rome and seized power, bringing Italy, and Pisa, under the Fascist yoke. Black Shirts took to parading in the Campo dei Miracoli.

Il Duce himself adored the Campo dei Miracoli; he reveled in its scale and calculated grandeur, and was envious of the power that had produced it. Like the Pisan Romanesque, the Fascist architecture promulgated by Mussolini—Milan's Stazione Centrale, the Casa del Fascio in Como, and the Foro Mussolini in Rome are examples—also looked to ancient Rome for inspiration, albeit reproducing it in a much-corrupted and hollow fashion. The only thing to irk the dictator about the Campo dei Miracoli, in fact, was the tower, an unfit symbol, in his mind, of a people with imperial ambitions. Hence, under the Mussolini regime, numerous commissions unsuccessfully confronted the campanile, until finally, in 1934, Mussolini seems to have decided that enough was enough: what the Tower of Pisa needed was not defeatists and academics, but men of action. The politics of consensus that had customarily characterized the commissions was abandoned for the simplicity of Fascist decree. In opposition to the informed opinion of nearly every expert in Italy as well as abroad, Mussolini personally authorized an ill-conceived plan conjured by the engineer Giulio Fascetti, which called for cement to be injected into the tower's foundation. For close to a year, workers pumped more than ninety tons of

Seaman apprentice Robert Bradford, of Chicago, Illinois, holds up the Leaning Tower of Pisa, January 6, 1948.

liquid cement into 361 holes drilled into the base of the tower. The intention, of course, was to solidify the tower's foundation in the terrain and to stop the flow of water that was deteriorating the subsoil beneath the campanile. The result, however, couldn't have been more contrary. Over the course of the eight months immediately following this latest intervention, the tower scarcely stopped moving in an erratic dance, first to the southeast, then to the north, south, east, and back again. The movements were seemingly minuscule, measured in millimeters or fractions thereof, but for the Tower of Pisa, such random motion was very nearly fatal. Eventually, the campanile came to rest almost precisely where it had stood before the cement intervention, as if it had found its old, habitual place despite the bullying of men.

Nearly eight centuries of shifting ground, architectural polemics, aggressive diagnoses, misguided remedies, earthquakes, floods, and Fascist designs were insufficient preparation for what the Tower of Pisa would have to endure during World War II. Pisa and the campanile hadn't witnessed a true war since the early sixteenth century, when Florence had besieged the city for the last time. Now, modern warfare was at the city's gates.

Using Sicily as a bridge to the mainland, just as the Saracens had done a thousand years before, the Allies undertook their Italian campaign in 1943, and with it Pisa assumed an importance it hadn't known for centuries. The city's beachhead and its half dozen bridges spanning the

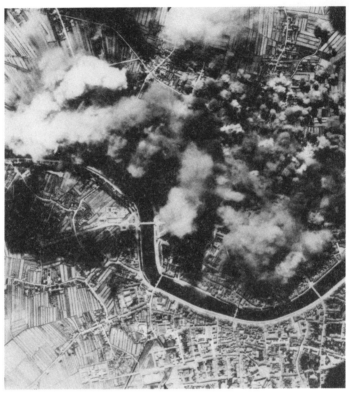

Allied bombers strike a German-occupied Pisa, September 11, 1943.

Arno suddenly became the objects of ferocious Axis defenses and the target of relentless Allied bombing, and the campanile stood squarely in the crossfire. Perhaps understandably, no one gave too much thought to the bell tower or any other monument in these years when the future of Europe hung in the balance.

By the summer of 1944, Allied troops had pushed north on the Italian peninsula, suffering unspeakable casualties but managing to successively take Naples, Montecassino, Rome, Civitavecchia, and Leghorn. In late July, the U.S. Ninety-first Infantry Division had forced German troops under Field Marshal Albert Kesselring to retreat to Pisa and the north bank of the Arno, and there the battle stalled. The marshy terrain around Pisa was hell for the infantry, and German troops were dug in. Despite the lack of natural high ground from which to direct their artillery fire, the Germans were shelling U.S. troops with uncanny accuracy. The only possible vantage point from which the Germans could have been spying Allied forces was the bell tower, christened the "tiltin' Hilton" by the American troops. It was then that a young American sergeant named Leon Weckstein entered the stage, and, for a moment at least, held the fate of the Tower of Pisa in his sights. He described his experience in his account of the campaign, *Through My Eyes: The 91st Infantry Division in the Italian Campaign* (Hellgate, 1999):

It must have been about 10:00 P.M. that night when I heard someone shout, "Sergeant Weckstein, the colonel wants to see you."

I double-timed it from my slit trench to the battalion command post about sixty yards away. "Sir?" I saluted, waiting for his attention.

"Sergeant, the general wants you to take a radio

man and leave at the crack of dawn tomorrow. Get yourself as close as you can to that tower. Stay within the cover of the olive groves, but for God's sake, be careful. Try to watch out for mines.

"We think the Germans are using it for an observation post," he continued. "Too damn many casualties. You might have to level it." He paused.

"We've got our cannon company, a couple of batteries of 105s and 155s already zeroed in for maximum effect, and even a destroyer offshore ready to help with their big, six-inch guns, if you need it." His repeated use of the pronoun *you* gave me a hint at what would come next. He continued in his usual understated tone of voice. "If you see anything that looks at all suspicious, don't wait. Call down fire."

Weckstein and the company's radio technician, Sergeant Charles King, moved out at dawn. The morning was hot and hazy, and it took the two men what seemed like an eternity to reach an olive grove about three-quarters of a mile from the campanile. Sergeant Weckstein trained his telescope on the tower in search of the enemy:

I carefully focused first on the highest point, the broad circular campanile of the tower. I could easily make out the shadowy silhouette of the old bells, quiet now, but nothing moved. I took my time training the scope ever so slowly up, down, and across each elaborately ornamented balustrade, attempting to discern anything that might be hidden within those black recesses and arches.

For a moment, I indulged my senses. Somewhat hypnotized by the awe-inspiring tower and its artistic mastery, I tacitly noticed the elegance and grace it was really meant to convey. Momentarily, I dismissed the cunning enemy who most probably had been using it to wreak havoc on our troops, yet I knew that, if even a mouse dared scamper within my sight, my brief musing would cease immediately. . . . The words, "This is Abel George One. Fire!," would have been enough.

The morning sun grew hotter by the minute as my mind leaped back into reality. I looked again, this time with no need for further aesthetic gratification. I indulged myself in hoping against hope for even the slightest sign of a possible target. Then, to my utter amazement and chagrin, the marble tower suddenly turned into a vibrating mass of white, quivering gelatin, undulating crazily in a rapidly pulsating kind of dance.

I hadn't counted on such intense heat waves. No one had. This unexpected stumbling block completely thwarted my ability to focus. . . .

I ached with a desire to grab it, to take a firm hold with my bare hands and steady the convulsive thing. If only I could be allowed even the slightest suspi-

American Lieutenant General Mark Clark, Commander of the Fifth Army, and Major General Willis D. Crittenberger look over the town of Pisa just after it fell to the Allies, September 6, 1944.

cion, the slightest reason, to give the order to fire. Finish the damn job!

. . . But it was the enemy who had the advantage of the blazing sun that morning. Then it happened. . . . The sky directly above us suddenly exploded with ear-splitting bursts of black smoke. Sergeant King and I became the very unwilling recipients of a hail of horrendous shrapnel that began to rain down all around us. With no overhead protection from the log we had used for cover, we could only retreat as fast as possible and dodge the hot, metal sleet that followed us.

As we moved swiftly and dodged through the trees, King radioed back that our position had become untenable. Amidst the crackling sound of static, we received a most disconcerting but welcome reply from Sergeant Brown back at the command post.

"Get your asses out of there! The friggin' generals have decided to spare the tower anyhow. Come on back."

It is no small irony that most of the men who have tried to rescue the campanile over the centuries have turned out to come closest to destroying it, and that two American sergeants who had been sent out on a mission that could potentially have blown the tower sky high instead became some of the few men in history who actually managed to save it.

When the first American troops finally entered the Campo dei Miracoli on September 2, 1944, they found a ruinous, pockmarked square, but the duomo, the baptistery, and the campanile had gone unscathed. In fact, the only damage suffered by the Tower of Pisa during the whole war was inflicted by friendly fire when in 1943 an Italian antiaircraft gun mistakenly shot at the campanile and destroyed a third-story column. The Camposanto was not so lucky. During the fierce battle for Pisa, an American incendiary grenade landed in the monumental cemetery and tragically destroyed irreplaceable works by Benozzo Gozzoli, Andrea Orcagna, and Spinello Aretino. Otherwise, the Campo dei Miracoli emerged from the devastation as if, well, by a miracle, and the Tower of Pisa found itself enveloped in the mystique of an edifice that neither gravity nor earthquakes, neglect or even war, could topple.

NINE

Step This Way, Signore e Signori

"A little more to the right, honey, a little more, that's it.
Now, raise your arms and pretend that you're holding up
the tower. Right there! Now smile . . . perfect! Oh, the
folks are going to love this!"

—Camera-wielding American tourist to her husband,
Campo dei Miracoli, summer 2000

On June 16, 2001, the feast of St. Ranieri, Pisa's patron saint, a multitude gathered beneath the campanile to celebrate the completion of the most recent works to restore and stabilize the tower. Among the rather high proportion of dignitaries were the minister of public works as well as the mayor, the president of the Opera Primaziale Pisana, and the archbishop and his entourage. Also in attendance were the fourteen members of the commission—the seventeenth so far—responsible for saving the Tower of Pisa, including its indisputable star, Professor John Burland of Imperial

College, London. Formations of soldiers in medieval Pisan garb, bearing daggers, swords, muskets, and pikes, struck a festive note as they stood guard around the tower and the duomo. Locals and tourists milled about the square. From the summit of the campanile, the Pisan standard, a white cross on a red field, flew against a flawless Tuscan sky.

The festivities began with a brief prayer, followed by a good many speeches, a bit of music, and an awards ceremony in which the members of the commission were presented by the city with medals of distinguished merit. When Professor Burland returned the key of the campanile to the authorities of the Opera della Primaziale in a symbolic gesture indicating that the commission had fulfilled its task and that the tower was once again in civic hands, the crowd burst into spontaneous cheers, rejoicing at the end of an eleven-year ordeal in which their beloved campanile had been closed, subject to relentless tests and experiments, nearly toppled, all but abandoned, and finally saved from certain ruin in the eleventh hour. The crowd was also justly applauding the commission itself, the same one that only a few years before had been ridiculed in the press and denounced in the cafés, salons, and streets of Pisa as costly, incompetent, and doomed. The applause had the ring, therefore, of an acquittal, as well it should have, for as nearly everyone gathered in the Campo dei Miracoli now knew, Burland and company had finally succeeded where so many others had roundly failed. In a phrase, Commis-

View of the cathedral through the columns of the tower

sione #17 had reversed the Tower of Pisa's centuries-old slide into oblivion.

Things had not always been so rosy for the group. After being disbanded on orders from Rome in late 1996, the seventeenth commission reconvened in Pisa in the autumn of 1997 in the aftermath of the Assisi earthquake. At that time, none of its members dreamed that one day they would be toasted in Pisa. The last time that they had intervened in tower affairs, two years before, these experts of the seventeenth commission had almost toppled it. Now they were back, and even though the time for half measures was clearly over, no one seemed overly eager to propose radical solutions for fear of becoming the campanile's executioner. Not that it mattered much: it was nearly impossible to achieve any semblance of a consensus on any plan of action, given that the commission included engineers from distinct fields, art historians, and architects, all working, it seemed, at cross purposes. Then Professor Burland and fellow commission member and engineer Carlo Viggiani argued for a process known as soil extraction, or soil subsidence. The procedure called for earth to be excavated from beneath the foundation on the north side of the tower in order to gently coax the structure back toward the perpendicular. Burland had successfully used the technique in his intervention in the metropolitan cathedral in Mexico City, and there was no reason why the procedure could not be applied to the campanile, at least in theory. However, from a practical standpoint, the process was expensive, time consuming, and not without considerable risks, among them the reality that one could never be completely sure of just how the *terreni limosi* might react. But in the final analysis, the plan was the Tower of Pisa's best hope for survival. Not to act would be to condemn the campanile to a death foretold.

For the better part of three years, then, Professor Burland prepared a soil extraction scenario for the campanile. He created computer models, subjected the terrain to exhaustive analyses, and finally built scale models of the tower in both aluminum and concrete. Every trial conducted by Burland and his colleagues proved a success; they learned, in effect, how to extract soil such that they could manipulate the movements of the models at will. Still, there were skeptics, even among their fellow commission members. Meddling in the terrain in the past had only caused the campanile hardship, and it was difficult to convince many, Pisans among them, that this new subterranean drilling technique was going to be any different. In the end, though, it was the locals who pressured the commission to give the green light to Burland's intervention. Although much of Pisa had been hostile to the commission's efforts from the start, they were growing increasingly impatient with the confusion that had kept their campanile closed for years on end and was costing the city incalculable losses of tourist revenue. They wanted action. By the autumn of 1999, it was time to put the plan—and the campanile—in motion.

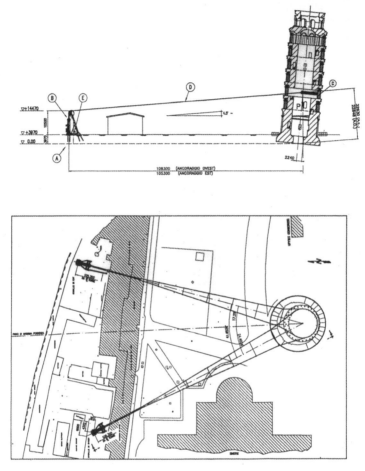

PLANIMETRIA STRALLATURA

A plan of the official project to stabilize the tower involving
removal of earth from the north side, June 17, 2000

Burland's initial intervention played out like a dream. With specially designed drills, he and workmen bored holes five meters deep into the terrain on the north side of the tower, and ever so slowly, soil from beneath the catino was extracted. The tower responded in kind: after a month, the top of the tower had moved back toward the perpendicular by five millimeters. While that figure may have struck most as insignificant, for Burland, Viggiani, and others who had bet on soil extraction, five millimeters represented a measure of unprecedented proportions. For the first time in eight centuries, the Tower of Pisa had taken a step in the right direction.

In time, more than sixty tons of *terreni limosi* were extracted from beneath the campanile, and the 14,700-metric-ton-structure moved 40.6 centimeters, or 0.5 degrees, back toward perpendicular. The seventh cornice now overhung the base by only four meters, the same as it had back in 1838 before the disastrous intrusion of Gherardesca. The Tower of Pisa, Burland ventured to say upon completing work, would be safe for another three hundred years.

With the tower secure, tourists flocked back to the Campo dei Miracoli. For in the end, it's the Leaning Tower of Pisa that they have always come to see. They dutifully visit the duomo, circle the baptistery, and glance at the splendid frescoes in the Camposanto, but in the shadow of the campanile they gasp and stare and linger and ponder in awe and disbelief. By a twist of fate, the

Stereoscopic view of the Leaning Tower and the duomo, by Under-wood & Underwood

campanile has become the indisputable protagonist in the square, and one of the most frequently visited historic monuments and tourist attractions in a country chock-full of both. It is ironic that a campanile built to glorify Pisan wealth and power has itself become the city's most cherished asset, its golden calf, as it were.

The Tower of Pisa, of course, is far more than a mere stop on the Tuscan tourist trail. It is a singular, skewed monument of incalculable aesthetic wealth and beauty that has become part of our collective consciousness. The campanile's preservation is not only a sound economic decision or a cultural obligation, but a moral imperative. Without the Tower of Pisa, our architectural landscape would be poorer, and so too our spirits. The image of this tilting, defiant campanile symbolizes all that is wondrous and strange in a world that is fast losing good measures of both. In the end, the Tower of Pisa eluded the sad fate of the lighthouse at Alexandria, the colossus of Rhodes, and the hanging gardens of Babylon, and it narrowly escaped the ranks of wonders of the world lost.

Illustration Credits

About the Author

NICHOLAS SHRADY is the author of *Sacred Roads: Adventures from the Pilgrimage Trail.* His articles have appeared in *Architectural Digest, The New York Times Book Review, Travel & Leisure, Forbes,* and *Town & Country.* Since 1986, he has made his home in Barcelona. His wife, Eva Ortega, and his sons divide their time between Barcelona and their olive grove in the hills above the Ebro Delta.